D0975489

"*Malham has shared with the rest of the world the mystique of the incredible cj Advertising culture that every business needs to know and learn from. If you want a culture that produces passion, fun, creativity, and is all about the customer, read this book. Have all your people read this book.*"

—JOHN R. DIJULIUS III, author, *The Customer Service Revolution*

"*Finally! A book without theory and concepts. Arnie Malham supplies market-proven tactics that build a winning business culture.* Worth Doing Wrong *is the playbook for profits with a smile.*"

—JACK DALY, best-selling author, *Hyper Sales Growth*

WORTH

DOING

WRONG

WORTH

The Quest to Build a Culture That Rocks

DOING

ARNIE S. MALHAM

WRONG

Published by Advantage, Charleston, South Carolina.
Member of Advantage Media Group.

ADVANTAGE is a registered trademark and the Advantage colophon is a trademark of Advantage Media Group, Inc.

Printed in the United States of America.

ISBN: 978-1-59932-587-3
LCCN: 2016948659

Cover design by George Stevens.

This publication is designed to provide accurate and authoritative information in regard to the subject matter covered. It is sold with the understanding that the publisher is not engaged in rendering legal, accounting, or other professional services. If legal advice or other expert assistance is required, the services of a competent professional person should be sought.

 Advantage Media Group is proud to be a part of the Tree Neutral® program. Tree Neutral offsets the number of trees consumed in the production and printing of this book by taking proactive steps such as planting trees in direct proportion to the number of trees used to print books. To learn more about Tree Neutral, please visit **www.treeneutral.com.**

Advantage Media Group is a publisher of business, self-improvement, and professional development books and online learning. We help entrepreneurs, business leaders, and professionals share their Stories, Passion, and Knowledge to help others Learn & Grow. Do you have a manuscript or book idea that you would like us to consider for publishing? Please visit **advantagefamily.com** or call **1.866.775.1696.**

TABLE OF CONTENTS

FOREWORD
BY JOE CALLOWAY

You can't *not* have a culture.

Think about that.

Culture is my hot button. I believe that culture is the primary reason for the success or failure of most businesses. That's why it's vitally important for you to realize that you can't *not* have a culture.

You have a culture, and it's running your business right now.

The question is this: Is your culture by default or by design?

The biggest failure of most business leaders is that they aren't intentional about their companies' cultures. They've just let a culture *happen*. The leaders of these companies stay awake at night wondering why, with the people and resources they presently have, they aren't doing better.

Here's why: it's culture.

Fix it, and you'll do better—way better.

It takes a *lot* of work to build the right culture, but it's worth the work, because if you don't get culture right, you're going to fail. If, however, you do build and sustain a culture that works, you will almost certainly succeed.

That's a pretty bold statement, and I make it with absolute confidence.

I've got over thirty years' experience in studying why companies succeed and fail, and in passing those lessons along to the business world through my books, consulting, and speaking at corporate events. I also owned a restaurant for ten years and am presently involved in two start-ups (a snowboard company and an entertainment company), and I'm a partner in a real estate development company.

Business endeavors will do well or go bust for any number of reasons, but if we don't get culture right in each of them, they don't stand a chance.

Because I write books on business success, I know how many of them are out there. The list is endless. If you're in a bookstore right now, and you picked up this book just to take a look, I know full well that you've got hundreds of other choices right in front of you. If you go home and go to amazon.com, they offer 1,565,878 books on business. There are books on leadership, management, motivation, process, infrastructure, systems, planning, communication . . . it goes on forever.

Trust me, this is the one. This is the book.

You're about to read something that can change everything. I assure you that I'm choosing those words with absolute intention: *this book can change everything.*

You don't have to do it exactly the way Arnie did it in his business, although my personal opinion is that the way he did it is about as good as it gets. But, as Arnie says in the book, *do something.*

Because I'm an author and speaker and I've had some success at it, people sometimes quote me.

. . . I quote Arnie Malham.

After reading this book, I'm going to be quoting him a lot more.

To me, the ideas in this book are so compelling that they transcend "Why would we do this?" They come under the category of "Why in the world *would we not* do this?" You have no good reason not to begin to make your culture rock—beginning now.

The beauty and power of Arnie's message about culture is that it's so simple. That's not to say that it's easy. It takes a ton of work and a lot of courage to do the kinds of things that Arnie's done with cj Advertising.

But it's not complicated. It just boils down to whether or not you choose to do it.

Read Arnie's book, take a deep breath, find your courage, and do it. You'll look back on it as one of the best decisions you ever made.

It's worth doing wrong.

—Joe Calloway, author, *Be the Best at What Matters Most*

Arnold A. Malham
1927–2008

ACKNOWLEDGMENTS

I compulsively make lists for a great number of things. This is my "But Not For" list of people who've made me who I am. Whenever I got it wrong, they helped me get it right. This book is dedicated to them.

Arnold A. Malham, my father.

Lynda Fitzhugh, my sister, who saved me from drowning at age six.

Isaac Malham, my uncle, who taught me respect, religion, and how to shoot pool.

Reverend Jim McDaniel, a hometown minister, who taught me "the turtle always wins."

Jack Burrell, my high school football coach, who believed I could compete.

Patrick Redfearn, the driver of the Blazer, who struggles occasionally with advanced math.

Bela Chain, my college fraternity advisor, who was instrumental in my graduating.

Jerry McCoin, my fraternity little-brother's father, who introduced me to Nashville's legendary **Ralph Brown**, who introduced me to **Paulette Whitworth**, Nashville's first female banking VP, who introduced me to **Dana McClendon**, the then president of First American National Bank, who offered me my first job in Nashville.

Martha Elzen, my boss at First American National Bank, who taught me how to analyze data for outliers.

Tom Ervin, who hired me at WTVF NewsChannel 5 in 1990, **Neil Schwartz**, who was my first boss, and **Bob Neil**, who took away my guaranteed salary within six months and forced me to learn consultive selling.

Ellen Moore, my first solo sale at WTVF and **Stephanie Goff**, my largest direct client.

Lem Lewis, GM of WTVF, following Tom Ervin, who taught me the power of lunch at Krystal's.

Kathy Himelberg, my second boss at WTVF, who introduced me to my bride and was then forced to fire me (my fault, not hers).

Anne Gorton Malham, my bride (since 1995), who opened my mind and heart to a much bigger and more beautiful world.

J. Marshall Hughes, the first legal client of cj Advertising, who taught me "the more you know, the more you can help."

Bill Berg, cj Advertising's second legal client, who taught me to "always do what I say I'm going to do."

Bob Crumley, cj Advertising's third and, eventually, largest legal client, who taught me the power of perpetual growth.

Jimmy Bewley, my business partner and best friend.

Verne Harnish, founder of EO, author of *Scaling Up*, and business thought leader who has always championed my story and fed my growth mind-set.

Carter Mario, significant agency client, who pushes us hardest toward success.

Chris Stovall, my company's COO, who makes the noise go away.

My EO Forum Six: **Andy Bailey, Clay Blevins, Sonny Clark, Steve Curnutte, Rob Frankfather, Joe Freedman, David Waddell,** and all past and future members.

David Rumsey who took a web of notes, half stories, and half chapters; and helped turn them into the book you are holding. Without his help, this book does not happen. Thank you, Dave! You Rock!

Yes, there are more, so many more, who have made me a wiser and more enlightened person and to whom I am forever grateful: my mom, **Sada Marie Malham**; my younger sister, **Lisa Malham Kessler**; my children **Brick** and **Sydney Malham**; my best friend on four legs, **Katy Malham**; my high school partners in crime: **Michael Oxner, Joel McDaniel,** and **Todd Ray**; and my Ole Miss crew: **Herbie Hess, Keith Lockhardt, Brad Biddy, Doug Wright,** and **Scott Turner**, just to name a few.

INTRODUCTION

Ask the average person, "What's the most important ingredient in achieving sustainable business success?"

1. Ideas

2. Execution

3. Culture

I'll bet most of the population will say ideas are the most important, execution the next most important, and culture the least important.

I happen to believe the exact opposite is true. I believe that culture trumps both ideas and execution in terms of creating a sustainable and successful business. Culture allows for the machine to actually work and, when it breaks, to be fixed and keep moving. Give me a company with a bunch of ideas and bad culture and poor execution, and I'll show you a company that's headed for bankruptcy. I would challenge the greatest researchers in the world to find a company that runs optimally (or even adequately) without putting culture first. Culture is what creates great execution that allows companies to harvest their ideas. Great businesses are created through great culture.

The least valuable aspect of a company's success is its ideas. If you don't have the gumption to create a culture that actually executes them, you've got nothing. Take Starbucks, for example. Prior to the coffee boom, any businessperson (or even nonbusinessperson) would've told you that selling $4 coffee was a spectacularly bad idea. But Starbucks did it by creating a culture so bold, invigorating, and inviting that it actually revolutionized the entire consumer experience of drinking coffee in America. Sure the coffee is delicious, but the Starbucks culture tastes even better. Just do a cursory web search about the importance of culture at Starbucks. It'll blow your mind.

I love talking about Starbucks because it reminds me of another bad idea: my business. To a lot of people I've met, my business is a really bad idea. Ready for it? I run an ad agency that exclusively services law firms. Personal…injury…law firms. Sound a little crazy? A little too niche for your taste? Well, guess what? We may not be Starbucks, but by every standard used to measure business success, we're a smash hit. Client satisfaction, employee satisfaction, sustained growth, longevity, profits, expansion, awards, and publicity—it's all there, and it's all attributable to a culture that rocks.

In this book, I'm going to tell you how I grew a culture that turned my bad idea into a business adventure that has lasted for over twenty years. I'm going to give you examples of how we continue to emphasize and work on our culture. You'll love some of our methods; you'll feel shocked and repelled by others. But I promise you—all of our crazy ideas work for us, and I hope they'll inspire you to generate culture-building initiatives that work for you. The specific examples I give in this book represent larger concepts that can be applied to any business or department. Whether you're a butcher, a banker, or a candlestick maker, culture is vital to your success. And if you're neglecting it, you're not succeeding at the level you should be.

CULTURE: IT'S SO IMPORTANT IT'S WORTH GETTING WRONG

My mantra and title of this book is, "If it's worth doing, it's worth doing wrong," which means that most progress happens when you get it wrong. Here's an example. Back before GPS, when I got lost, I got *good* and lost. But by the time I figured out where I was, I really knew my way around. The same is true in business. In building spreadsheets and looking at data, it's the outlier that often explains everything. Finding the piece that's wrong can be the key to the entire puzzle.

Culture is the ultimate "worth-getting-wrong" strategy. Like a garden (and I hate gardening), culture can't be perfect and needs constant attention. It's better to put a little work into it than none. It's better to put a lot of work into it than just a little. Everything you do for the sake of improving your culture is good.

If you wait and do it perfectly, you may never do it. And if you never do it, it can get out of control. Do it; do it wrong; make it better; make it right. Be willing to make the mistakes (as we are). Be willing to move forward (as we have).

If you can't commit to actually doing this—changing the way you run your workplace—stop reading now. It does you no good to know all this stuff if you're not going to implement it. You can't just read or talk about improving your culture. You actually have to *do* it. You've got to be willing to try things that everyone around you will say won't work. You've got to be willing to get it wrong on your way to getting it right.

If it's worth doing, it's worth doing wrong.

RIP OFF AND DUPLICATE

The road to getting it right is not smooth or without detours. Fortunately, there are plenty of smart people out there who've traveled it ahead of me. When people ask me how I came up with ideas for creating a great culture, my answer is "R&D: rip off and duplicate." I'm not ashamed to tell you. I take whatever I can get from other people and retool it to make it work for me. Throughout this book, you will see credits to others. (By the way, one of the best things I ever

R&D'd is that line itself, which came directly from Cameron Herold, the rock star Founder of BackPocket COO. Thanks, Cameron!)

Let me be clear. This is not the "all-your-answers-are-in-this-book" book. I realize I'm taking a risk saying that in the introduction because you might be tempted to ask, "Then why should I continue reading?" But the truth is that business is hard, and all these things are just ideas that might, just might, make it a little easier. This is not a how-to book. It's a how-to-think book. Please rip off and duplicate freely.

CHAPTER ONE

TAKE CARE OF YOUR CULTURE (BEFORE IT TAKES CARE OF YOU)

It's alive! Whether you like it or not, your culture is a living, breathing thing. Deprive your company's culture of nourishment, and it will start hunting for food. In fact, the more you neglect your culture, the more out of control it gets. Ever witness the destructive power of water-cooler gossip? That is company culture, fighting for its own survival and morphing into something toxic right under your nose. You could have a great business idea with an equally sound plan to execute it. But trust me when I tell you a corrosive culture *will* rot your infrastructure and prevent your plan from working.

That's what was happening to my company.

We're an ad agency that markets law firms—and lots of 'em. We have clients all across the USA and in Canada. About nine years into this journey, I was still struggling to sustain momentum. After some serious soul searching, I realized I had two huge challenges. Here's a clue as to what they were. When I talked to a prospective hire, this was the typical conversation:

"Hi, I'm Arnie Malham. I own and run an advertising agency."

"That's sounds interesting, are you hiring?"

"I'm always looking for good people."

"I'd love to work for an ad agency. It's like *Mad Men*, right?"

"Yes. It's sorta like *Mad Men*."

"What kind of work do you do?"

"We create TV Ads, build websites, design Billboards, and create content that builds legal brands."

"Legal Brands?"

"Yes Lawyers."

"What kind of lawyers?"

"Personal Injury Lawyers"

"Oh…but you do work for other types of business right?"

"No…we are completely focused on building brands for personal injury lawyers."

"Oh…No, I don't want to work for that kind of agency."

Boom! The shine was off the apple. It's pretty obvious that my two big problems were recruitment and retention. No A-level writer, producer, editor, project manager, or designer dreams of working in an agency that serves personal injury (PI) attorneys. This isn't to disparage what attorneys do. I believe lawyers level the playing field and serve a purpose in our economy and in our justice system. When you watch movies such as *Erin Brockovich*, *A Civil Action*, or *The Rainmaker*, you cheer for the lawyer! That's not the point. The point is I had a business to run and clients to serve, and I needed quality people to help me. Initially, my neglect of our culture had been masked by the euphoria of owning a young start-up. But after a few years, the honeymoon was over (more on that later). You enter that second stage of your business, and stuff starts gettin' real. I needed to attract top new talent and retain the good folks we already had. In a town such as Nashville, where there are a lot of opportunities for creative people, recruitment and retention were battles we were losing. I've actually had people tell me, "I don't want you on my résumé." Ouch! And if that's what people were telling me to my face, imagine what they were saying to others. I was feeling the effects of a culture gone bad. I knew I needed to do something but couldn't figure out what.

CULTURE REFLECTS LEADERSHIP

In 2007 world renowned customer service consultant John DiJulius visited our offices to give a presentation to all of our clients and staff. He said these magic words: "Culture reflects leadership."

It was as if a jolt of electricity had rippled through me. I thought, *Whoa! It's* my *fault that I don't have the culture that I want.* Hiring the right people (though part of the solution) was not the first step to fixing my culture. I had to create the culture I wanted to attract the right people. And so I began working on growing a culture by design rather than by default, one that allowed us to be who we were and let those attracted to our organization see the world the way I see it.

My goal through all of this has been to create a culture and a company that looks so good on a résumé that any other agency or company would want to hire my staff on the spot. If you're hiring in the hotel business, and a candidate who spent four years at the Ritz-Carlton applies for the job, you're going to hire them, right? You'd be crazy not to. If you work in retail and have candidates who worked for Neiman Marcus, the Container Store, or Zappos for five years, you'd hire them because they understand retail. That's what I was aiming for. I wanted outsiders to see that people from my agency understood how to service clients, how to make work fun, how to be productive, and how to be accountable. I wanted to be known for developing talented people who are of good character. When my staff members were at a bar, restaurant, church, or party and someone asked them, "Where do you work?" I wanted them to be able to respond with stories about how great work was at my company. I wanted their answer to make the other person want to work for my company.

I thought hard about my company and asked myself what we could do to make our culture remarkable. We changed our approach to culture from one that's accidental to one that's intentional. Our goal was to grow from being an average place to work to being an outstanding place to work. It took a lot of effort, a ton of fun, and a hefty amount of R&D.

It's paid off big time!

Here is a list of everything we've ever done in order to grow our culture. Some of it's going to scare you, piss you off, or make you laugh. That's fine. It's not your company; it's my company. But I guarantee you, for every one of my cultural initiatives that's a great fit for us, there's a parallel initiative that is a good fit for you. As you read this list, think about your company or department and what you could be doing within your own business.

NOTE: A few of these items have been discontinued, but the *vast majority* of them are still working well. *All* of it was worth getting wrong.

MY KIND OF CULTURE

- unrestricted paid time off

- surprise beer cart (Yes, we hand out beers at work.)

- casual dress

- dog friendly

- kid friendly

- BetterBookClub (We pay people to read.)

- free postage for personal mail
- Sonic ice machine
- theater popcorn maker
- morale surveys
- Dream Manager: program to help employees accomplish their personal dreams
- employee-run morale team
- results-only work environment (ROWE)
- NHL hockey ticket drawings
- birthday gift cards for team members and their immediate family (but *no* birthday cake)
- free fruit
- free mints
- themed work days
- themed work weeks
- rockin' break room
- referral bonuses
- profit-sharing annual bonuses
- make-your-day gift cards
- anniversary swag
  - five-year company jackets
  - ten-year anniversary Rolexes
  - fifteen-year anniversary trips

- employee-of-the-month recognition
- Camels with a Cause: philanthropy program
- camel mascot
- hump day quote: inspiration e-mailed every Wednesday
- word of the day
- cj client annual conference
- rockin' holiday party
- staff meeting-day bagels
- meetings that inspire
  - monthly staff meetings
  - standing huddles
  - town hall meetings
- peer performance reviews
- celebrate success
  - thank-you cards
  - peer recognition envelopes
  - daily rockers
  - monthly rockers
- sixty-day contract and employment confirmation
- first-day welcome baskets
- welcome lunches for new employees
- free parking
- free coffee

- free lunch with the boss (monthly)
- cool company swag
- community umbrellas and ponchos
- gourmet food trucks in the parking lot
- quarter sodas
- YMCA membership discounts
- department outings
- quiet time (no meetings from 1:00 p.m. to 2:00 p.m.)
- transparency with financials, strategy, and operational KPIs
- Wii in the break room
- aggressive and proactive training for every team member
- confidential cash advances (no questions asked)

Whew! This list is so long even I am freaked out a little bit when I see it all at once. Don't worry; it wasn't accomplished all at once or by only one person. Nor does this list represent a finished master-piece. It's probably the middle (or is it the beginning?) of a big, hairy, audacious journey that will never end—and thank goodness because, bottom line, we've made our company a kick-ass place to work! Take a look at the return on our investment.

THE ROI OF A CULTURE THAT ROCKS

- **Helps achieve (smash) business goals.** Every crazy or sane thing we do has a purpose and contributes in a positive way to our bottom line. Beer on Fridays? Good for morale! Casual dress? Attracts creative self-starters! BetterBookClub? Educates our people, raises morale, and is an awesome perk for recruiting. Since we began making a concerted effort to improve our culture, we grew to become the largest ad agency and call center exclusively serving personal injury law firms in the nation.

- **Creates win-win relationships.** Our culture has enabled a healthy cohesiveness between leadership and the entire company, between the company and our customers. I love casual dress; so do they. I love dogs and kids; we're dog and kid friendly. People who don't get it don't want to work here. People who *do* get it love it and want to stay. Our clients feel that love. Win . . . win . . . win!

- **Generates buzz.** We've been voted one of the best places to work in Nashville. Our culture has been the subject of news stories. We regularly conduct tours for other entrepreneurs and managerial types who study our culture as if we were a zoo exhibit. The buzz helps recruitment and energizes our staff. It's called a positive feedback loop, and it's real.

- **It just rocks!** A good culture fosters a team environment that is self-starting, respectful, motivated, appreciative, and goal oriented. We are dominating a field that other folks might find tough to swallow, and we're having a blast doing it!

THE SEVEN COMMANDMENTS

First and foremost, a culture that rocks is a culture by design, not by default. You have to be proactive and grow the specific culture that *you* want. I've already acknowledged that our specific cultural initiatives may not be a good fit for you. If you have a mostly hourly workforce, "unrestricted paid time off" is probably a pretty irritating thing to read. If you're an investment banker, flip flops and tank tops (allowed by our casual dress code) are probably not going to project the image that inspires confidence.

But I also promised that each of our specific initiatives would point to a broader philosophical concept that is indispensable for success. After years of getting it wrong in order to get it right, I was able to identify those bigger ideas that all can use to improve their culture. You might consider them the seven commandments for creating a culture that rocks!

1. Respect your employees.

2. Invest in your employees.

3. Embrace top-down core values.

4. Hire for culture.

5. Generate unavoidable culture. (Go big or go home!)

6. Do it wrong, make it better, get it right.

7. Never give up.

See? Now, those don't sound so crazy, do they? Reread this list, and take a minute to reflect on each item. Then proceed with the rest of the book.

Business is hard.
Culture by design won't fix all your problems—
but it makes it worth doing wrong.

CHAPTER TWO

RESPECT YOUR EMPLOYEES

This is where it all starts. Respect is the cornerstone in building a culture that rocks. I believe this so strongly that respect is a core value for my company and for me. In our organization, we respect our team as a group, and we respect each person as an individual. Our expectation is that the more respect we give, the more respect we get. Respect doesn't have to be part of your company's core values, but it must be part of your culture.

LET PEOPLE CONTRIBUTE

It's rare that you have someone who comes to work and says, "I don't want to contribute. I don't want to be creative. I don't want to be part of the solution. Just tell me what to do, and I'll do it." People don't start their jobs saying, "I want to be relegated to useless." People start their job just as they start school or a relationship: with eyes wide open and arms outstretched, ready to contribute, to try new things, and to be challenged. But inevitably, that bright-eyed optimism is soured through bad leadership and toxic culture. Little by little, their spirit is crushed by comments (and nonverbal messages) such as "that's not how we do it here," "wait until you know more," "your opinion doesn't matter," and "that idea's no good." That kind of attitude snuffs out proactivity and kills innovation. Sooner or later, people stop trying.

In my experience, everyone has an urge to be creative or contribute to the workplace on some level. It's easy with the wrong kinds of culture to diminish or tamp down those desires. But why would you? You don't know where the next great idea is coming from. Ignoring your team is a waste of resources, like airline seats that go unsold, hotel room nights that can never be recovered, and the books you buy but never read. Chronic waste like this sours people on what you're about. Pretty soon the party gets quieter and quieter, and finally, no one is saying anything. The silence is deadly.

EMPOWER PEOPLE TO SPEAK

One of the most important ways you can show respect is by *listening*. Before you can do that, you have to create an environment that raises those voices and gets people excited about new ideas and willing to try new things, willing to get it wrong on their way to getting it right. Once you have one good idea, someone else has to have a better one. Then someone else has an even better idea, which propels someone else to have an even better idea. Pretty soon, the spirit of innovation is propelling itself. Then the quiet lifts, and the murmur becomes a roar. That's the culture that wins.

How does this play out in our company? Say that we need to come up with a commercial for one of our clients. We start out by looking at all their competition in the market. We compare that to our own work. Then we roll up our sleeves to try and find a better idea. How do you get to a better idea? You brainstorm it. It's been shown through research that improvisation sparks areas of the mind that are otherwise unattainable in the normal thought process. The comics that are great at improv are actually using a part of their brain that, typically, isn't used. They get into this rhythm in which spontaneous creativity flows out of them. In sports it's called *being in the zone*, where the part of the brain that makes you tentative and careful shuts down, and the part of the brain that instinctively knows what to do fires up. (See *The Rise of Superman: Decoding the Science of Ultimate Human Performance* by Steven Kotler.) When you're not thinking about thinking, that's when you are really thinking! It happens in meetings too, because you're getting from one idea to another, and it's rolling faster and faster. All of a sudden you're getting a higher intellectual result because all the meeting participants trust each other and flow off each other.

The innovative spark can't exist without trust, and creativity can't flow through a wall of fear. If you're going to reap the benefits of listening to your employees, you must ensure they feel empowered to speak. Most would agree that "the right culture fosters creativity." Maybe you're not in a creative field, but every business needs creative thinking. That creativity should not be compartmentalized in brainstorms or isolated meetings; it should abound throughout your organization.

How do you make this happen? Watch the words you use. Things that get said in our meetings:

"I like that idea, tell me more about that."

"Let's explore that."

"What would happen if that were true?"

"How would that look?"

"Tell me more."

"Tell me more."

"Tell me more."

(I think I say, "tell me more" more than anything else.)

Things that *don't* get said:

"That's a dumb idea."

"That'll never work."

"We tried that before."

Everyone has bad days. I have bad days. My staff has bad days. I'm sure there have been times when we've squelched ideas and hurt people's feelings. That said, it's not the norm. The Norm is, and must be, *respect*. All of the things that we do—welcoming people's dogs and kids, gifting their families, and celebrating their successes (both personal and professional)—are daily reminders to my team members that their contributions are valued, that I trust them to be at their best, and most importantly, that they have my respect.

MORALE SURVEY: DARK ARTS THAT BUILD TRUST

Remember you don't have a bad culture because you have bad people. You have bad culture because you're a bad leader. For me, the dawn broke when I realized that in order to reap the benefits of listening, I had to find a systematic way for people to give their input. I created a system I called a morale survey. Sounds simple right? Well, it's not. Morale surveys are very dark arts. I can't stress this enough. Don't try them if you're not willing to confront some serious demons—yours and everyone else's. Here's what I mean. In 2007, we started with the simple notion of getting a sense of our morale. I would bring into my office people who I thought were "in the know," and I'd ask them, "Tell me what's going on. Why is this guy so upset?" or "Why is that person angry?" My heart was in the right place, but all I did was create more problems. I'd hear what was happening, and I'd go try to fix it. Usually, that would just magnify the problems or stir up more rumors. Not good.

After getting it wrong, we decided to give anonymous surveys to the entire team. The survey asked, "Of any place you can imagine working, with a score of ten being best place you can imagine and one being the worst, how is your morale at this company, right now? Just circle a number, and write in why you chose that score."

At first, people were nervous about opening up. They'd type the answer or disguise their handwriting because they thought we were trying to catch them at something. Clearly, their thinking was, *I'm going to write something down, and you're going to tie it to me.* They thought it was a witch hunt. Eventually, everyone could see that we were honestly trying to do what was best for all. But first, we had to start small. People said they hated our coffee maker; we changed it. People asked for more information about benefits; we gave it to them. When someone complained the office was too hot, we turned down the thermostat. After a few surveys, the trust grew, and people really started to open up. The steady stream of honest feedback was incredible. So we kept doing it.

We were taking the temperature of our morale by calculating the average score and reading the comments. From the beginning, we felt it important to reply to every comment. Even if the comment were, "Everything's great!" we'd say, "Thanks!" If the comment were, "I really love my new computer," we'd say, "Good equipment is the cornerstone of good operations." We'd always say *something* to let them know they'd been heard. If they said, "I'm overworked and underpaid," we'd reply to that. If they said, "I heard you were going to fire half the staff next week," we'd reply to that. Every month, we posted the average score, the participation rate, and *every* comment along with its reply—every comment, every response.

Today our morale surveys are still going strong. We use a web-based survey to help us manage the data, but it's still as simple as one question, one response.

"On a scale of one to ten (ten being the best morale you could imagine in a work environment and one being the worst), how does cj rate? If your score is four or below, please include a comment."

cj Morale Score

Total comments received since March 2007 : 1827

8.14
May 2016 Score

82%
May 2016 Participation Rate

Since starting the morale surveys in 2007, monthly morale scores and participation rates have been updated and posted monthly in our war hall.

After the survey deadline, our leadership team reviews every comment. We average out the results and post that average on the wall along with the participation rate. We also respond via staff-wide e-mail to every comment. Finally, we post those comments and replies on our website. Every comment we've ever gotten and every reply we ever issued is on our website right now. (You can go read them at http://www.cjadvertising.com/about-us/our-culture/morale-surveys/.)

We publish everything to hold ourselves accountable and to make sure we speak the truth. Our only exception to the transparency rule is that personal attacks are not allowed. This is not a forum that tolerates bullying. Nobody (other than the boss) can be singled out either by name or by implied circumstance. In the rare instance when this occurs, we try to edit the comment in a minimal way that allows the heart of the complaint to be read and addressed.

The benefits of a morale survey are amazing. It opens up the baffles of, "Tell me how to make this place better." It can take even the fiercest complaint and turn it into a way to improve the work environment. We've read thousands of comments and given thousands of responses. Morale has gone up when we expected it to go down and down when we expected it to go up. But a track record of delivering a morale score and responding to the comments has shaped what our culture is today. This process takes all the water-cooler talk and puts it out in the open so that the truth can be dealt with and the exaggerations can be managed.

It's led us to making everything from the smallest of changes to the biggest of changes. One time, we were building out our new office, a thirty-thousand-square-foot building right across the street from our old location. We had bought a building, were tackling a total renovation, and were spending several million dollars trying to get it right. We had cut back on some internal things because, quite frankly, the expenses were starting to freak me out a little bit. When I got a complaint about those cutbacks, I responded with, "We have to cut back because of the new building."

And you know what my people told me? They said, "Look, that new building's great for you, but it's just another place to work for us. We're in cubicles here; we'll be in cubicles over there. We don't want to hear about how expensive your building is. We want whatever it is you didn't give us because you're building that new building."

They were right. I can't penalize others because I'm building a new building. I have to do it all. I have to accept that as an owner, as an entrepreneur, and as a businessperson. I have to take the responsibility that, sometimes, when I'm doing stuff that's really for me, it doesn't entitle me to penalize them. I wouldn't have learned that lesson without the morale survey. And that's just one example.

Morale surveys demand that you respect your team because every month there's a reality check. Believe me. Your team will keep you humble. Being heard is important. Find a way to let the people that support you speak without fear and in a way that you have to respond thoughtfully and without resentment for the comment in the first place. A mechanism such as a morale survey kills toxic water-cooler talk, and it'll push you to be a better boss. As an added bonus, you might actually learn something.

Interesting side note: I've told many people about our morale survey system. The most common response is, "We could never do that. Our people would just complain about their work and ask for things." Please, pause and think about that one for a minute.

LEADERS BEWARE

Here's a word of advice, leader. Whatever you do, don't read morale survey comments alone—ever. It's like black magic or exploring a dark cave: you need a buddy (or, as we've found, a room full of them). If you're in a leadership role, you will read things that will make your blood boil. You'll get so mad you're liable to start trying to put blame on the people who wrote them: *Why do they feel that way? Don't they understand that I'm trying to get this done? Why don't they understand?*

The answer is always, "Because I haven't told them." The answer is not them; it's me. When I say "me," I mean you *and* your leadership team. Your people feel that way because they don't understand. If the majority of people feel that way, it's because you're really miscommunicating (or in the case of most companies, *not* communicating at all). There are times when we feel we are doing everything we can to address an issue. So we'll say, "We are doing everything we can to resolve this problem, but we need your help too." Sometimes, our answer is, "You're right. We should never have done that. We are going to fix it by doing this." It is a way to make sure we know how my team feels and to let the team know we're taking action to make them feel better.

You have to have courage. This whole thing works if you relax, listen, and learn, not tense up, shut down, and react. I've found I can get very angry about comments, which is why I'll only review them in a group. Then you just have to trust the process. If you start it and stop it, you'd be better off not doing it. If you think you're going to censor out when someone calls you a son of a bitch, then you'd be better off not doing it because you start ruining your integrity. If you can't control your feelings or your desire to go on a witch hunt for whoever wrote that comment, don't start it.

The biggest lesson that young leaders have to learn is that their culture is exactly what they create. The greatest leap of faith they take to create a better culture is when they admit that they alone don't have all the answers. Building from this lesson is what a morale survey is made for.

MEETINGS THAT INSPIRE

An important component to a respectful culture that often gets overlooked is how you conduct your meetings. Make no mistake, meetings represent the personal interactions that are the very essence of culture, not just how you behave within those interactions but also your approach to the meeting itself. Are you prepared? Are you considerate of the time attendees have committed? Our most important meeting concept, exposed by Verne Harnish in his masterful recap of the habits of business titans in his original book *Rockefeller Habits* and its modern update *Scaling Up*, is the *daily huddle*, which is actually two fifteen-minute, standing meetings that take place back-to-back. First, we do departmental huddles across the company. Then, selected people from each department come to the big huddle, where the department representatives talk about stuff. The meetings are fast, productive encounters that quickly let everyone get aligned. Standing encourages participants to conduct a more efficient meeting. Everyone has a chance to share immediate concerns or priorities as well as opportunities to celebrate successes.

Here's a typical huddle: "Okay, the client we're talking about is X. What do you know about what's going on with this client?" Different divisions of the company will speak up. Everyone has a voice. If employees know something, they inform the others. If they hear something that sparks an idea, they pass it along. They're in and they're out. They're not getting comfortable. If the conversation gets too deep, someone will say, "Let's take that offline." There is a huddle lead, but the huddle lead talks least, just throwing out the topic and encouraging conversation.

At the end of the huddle, we ask, "Who rocks?" Then employees nominate other employees for the good work they've done since the last huddle and, ideally, how what they've done ties into our core values. Someone may say, "Adam rocks for embracing growth. He finished an unusual project for a client, and we got it out the door ahead of schedule." The huddle lead will say, "Adam rocks on three. One, two, three..." and everyone responds with, "Adam rocks!"

The Daily Rocker is announced in our e-mailed *Huddle Notes* so that the whole company can see that Adam rocks. We've been doing this for six years. We have charts that show, by year, all those who have rocked and every day they've rocked. A thoughtful intentional approach to your meetings allows people to speak, listen, and get aligned with priorities.

Don't miss the opportunity to end your huddles with a cheer. From little league to the big league, teams do it before taking the field. It will feel goofy the first time or two, but it will quickly become expected, appreciated, and inspiring.

PEER RECOGNITION

The Daily Rocker program is just the tip of the iceberg for an even more powerful concept that we use to foster respect. You want to talk about the ultimate way to encourage respect within your company? Put the power to reward "out there" in the hands of everyone. Our Daily Rocker is seldom a managerial recommendation. It is almost always one peer recognizing another peer. People like having their managers shine the spotlight on them, but they love the appreciation that comes from their teammates.

Whenever possible, we encourage that dynamic throughout our organization.

Our monthly staff meetings are like huddles on steroids. They take a little longer, and everything is magnified, including the way we recognize success. The highlight of every staff meeting is the Envelope Recognition program. I walk into the staff meeting with ten envelopes. There's $10 inside eight of the envelopes, $20 inside the ninth, and $100 inside the tenth. Based on recognition by peers, we hand out an envelope to ten different people and let those who nominated them give the reason they're being hailed. At the end of the meeting, the recipients get their pictures taken with their envelopes. Nobody looks inside till later, because the honor and mutual respect is so great. If they get $10 or even $20, they're happy, and if they get $100, they're really happy. It's fun, it's meaningful, and it shows them their efforts are valued. We've been doing the Recognition Envelope program for years because it gives us a chance to recognize, reward, and build trust across teams.

THANK-YOU CARDS AND ANNUAL REVIEWS

Thank-you cards and annual reviews represent opposite ends of the peer recognition spectrum, but these programs are equally important. Thank-you cards are like trophies at our company. On their first day, newcomers are given a stack of about twenty-five company-branded thank-you cards. When employees witness someone doing good, they write a quick thank-you note and leave it on the desk of the do-gooder. It sounds corny, but it's freakin' awesome. People will send cards for good effort, good results, good teamwork, a good attitude, a display of kindness, or just to brighten someone's day. Then the recipients decorate their cube or their office with notes of appreciation, as we encourage each other through the work we need to get done. That cross appreciation can often be louder and more meaningful than recognition from a boss.

The beauty of this phenomenon is that it has its own inertia. The momentum of seeing notes of appreciation and gratitude in other peoples' cubicles or offices is self-propelling. The messages can include:

- "Thanks for pitching in on the campaign. I know that you stayed late to get the graphics done."

- "Thanks for finishing the project on time."

- "Thanks for helping me do the presentation required."

- "Thanks for helping me carry the plant to my office."

- "Thanks for bringing in the brownies."

- "Thanks for listening to me when I was upset over this or that."

- "Thanks for bringing me a Coke."

One person who really enjoyed her recent education opportunity sent one to me that read, "Thanks for investing in me." People can accumulate a lot of cards. Most folks tape or pin their cards around their workspaces as a constant reminder of the positive energy in our culture. The two minutes it takes to write a thank-you note can inspire its recipient forever.

Thank-you cards are a great way to show a little appreciation. Peer reviews are a much larger matter. In our company, an employee's peers have a direct impact on that employee's salary. If any employee's peers don't think they're pulling their weight, they'll feel the outcome of that opinion in their raise. If their peers give them high marks, they'll get a nice bump. Here's how it works. When it comes time for the annual review, all employees are evaluated by their manager and a select group of their peers, who rate based on critical competencies and completion of goals for the year. Peer ratings count as one-third of the overall performance score. That rating is combined with the employee's manager's score, and the number that determines the percentage of pay raise is calculated. Our employees know that if they are good to their peers, their peers will be good to them. That's how respect works.

RESPECT IS A TWO-WAY STREET

Respect can be shown in a multitude of ways. Here's a biggie: trust. Flexibility of schedule means giving complete control of hours to the workforce whenever possible. For many jobs, it's not about being at a desk for a certain length of time; it's about getting a job done by a certain time. Don't confuse the two. In fact, we're in the middle of a great "get-it-wrong" philosophical shift called results-only work environment (ROWE). ROWE is a trending management paradigm that is gaining traction in the business world (www.gorowe.com). Basically, the goal of ROWE is to move away from the traditional stick-and-carrot method of motivating people to find the sweet spot between compensation and pride in doing good work. ROWE can manifest itself in several ways, such as flexible hours, time off, and opportunities to work from home. It's led us to give everyone *unrestricted paid time off.* That means that employees, from their first day, can take as much time off as they need, whenever they need it, as long as they're getting their work done. How committed are we to this? We no longer track personal time off (PTO) in any way. We have long since stopped trying to manage individual schedules and have seen much more success in focusing on the deadlines and the results themselves. In other words, as long as employees are doing great work and getting it done on time, we don't really care when, where, or how they do it. We trust and respect them to get it done.

If you're in a sales force that works on straight commission, give yourself a round of applause. You're already in a ROWE environment! If you're in an hourly situation, you'll need to find a way to innovate here. For us, we pay a guaranteed 40 hours in some situations and we've created a liberal "cover me" and "shift swap" concept in others. We've worked hard and blown up the status quo to find a way to offer more flexibility and show trust across the board.

Maintenance of equipment, premises, and property is my alternative way of letting my people know that I respect them. How clean the bathrooms are, how clean the kitchen is, where trash goes, where employees sit (or stand), what the offices smell like, what the temperature and overall comfort level are—these elements are all important to me. If you are going to spend eight to ten hours a day in our world, I respect you enough to make it the best world possible. Maybe you already have the nicest, cleanest, most awesome house in the world? Great! This'll be just like home. Maybe you live in a pigsty, but here, by every possible standard, it's gong to be nice. Our desks, our chairs, our computers—all the things we use every day—are functional and high end. You know which room has the worst furniture? Our conference room. We've got Office Depot discount chairs in there that cost $139. When they break, we get a new one. Our people get the good stuff. We respect ourselves enough to feel that we deserve to work in a nice, clean, and comfortable place.

I just came back from a business meeting in another company's conference room, where the chairs were the nicest I'd ever seen. But they're wasted in the conference room where they're getting used once a day. I went back to their frontline area and saw more duct tape on their chairs than leather. That's not right.

Respect your people by giving them an environment in which they feel comfortable and welcome, especially if you want them to respect your customers and each other. Our janitorial bill is a little higher but so are our morale scores. Yours will be too, with just a little attention to the details of your surroundings.

SHARE THE INFORMATION

Transparency is a hot buzzword in the news these days, especially in politics. If people think you're hiding information, their minds will think the worst. Don't hide information. Put it out there, and let the truth set your people free. If you're serious about improving respect in the workplace, make every effort to increase transparency. Lack of transparency = lack of trust (and lack of courage). But sharing, as they say, really is caring.

I'm often amazed at the amount of information and data companies track but don't share. I'm even more amazed (and appalled) at the data companies don't even care enough to measure.

What are they so afraid of? Why do they keep the numbers a secret? What mutiny do they think will ensue by sharing information? At cj Advertising, we're not a bank or a brokerage firm. We're a whack-a-doodle, creative ad agency, but we track (and share) stuff a lot of number crunchers would never think of. Why? So we can chart our performance, keep what works, and chuck what doesn't. That's what you should do. Publish it, publish it, publish it. Financials? Publish them. Employee comments? Publish them. Complaints? Publish them. Solve the problem of secrecy and water-cooler talk by just putting the truth out there. Head off confusion through clear communication. Support the basis of your strategic moves by showing the data that led you to your decision.

If one person forms an opinion about something and tells six people what he thinks, those six people have no choice but to believe that's the prevailing attitude. That's the bigger problem: *Biff told me that the boss is taking home millions of dollars and screwing us. He told me and five other people that, so it must be true.* I've practically turned my business ledger inside out for my entire company to see. I've never regretted it. Neither will you.

Business is hard.
A culture of transparency and respect make it better.

CHAPTER THREE

INVEST IN YOUR EMPLOYEES

Leaders, stop here and make a list of everything you're doing to help your employees grow. The shorter the list, the more *you* are the problem.

As we grow our businesses, most leaders function in them as some sort of practitioner. Occasionally, I hear, "I'm a real entrepreneur. I work *on* the business, not *in* the business." But most of the time, we allow ourselves to lapse into doing some of the minutiae, especially if it's something we think we are expert at. We get caught up in the day-to-day running of a department, helping a client, or overseeing projects. We get so caught up in these tasks that we forget the most important thing we're there to do: grow our people.

What are you doing to encourage your employees' growth? If you're just reading this book with a blank stare, it's not enough. If it's a short list, then just know that your competitor for talent (who is everybody else in business, by the way, not just your competitor in your sector) is doing more. What are the ten programs that you are going to start? I'm not talking about one hundred programs, but I'm not talking about just one, either. Who will be the champions of those programs? What are the key performance indicators (KPIs) of the success of these programs? How are you going to promote the fact that you have these programs?

You can't just offer this stuff and forget it. You have to make sure it's working, being used, and measured. You might be thinking, *But what if I grow my employees and they leave?* Well, that could happen, but what if you don't grow them and they stay? The worst situation is having employees who aren't growing. If they're not growing, you're not growing.

PUT YOUR MONEY WHERE YOUR MOUTH IS

We want people to be as educated as possible in their jobs. We want them to know more today than they knew yesterday and more tomorrow than they know today.

At our company, we invest up to $60,000 a year in educating our people. That's pretty substantial for a company our size. Over the past 10 years, we've spent over half a million. We feel so strongly about it that we even maintained this investment during the recession, when a lot of companies were quick to slash training. Most importantly, we track and measure these events. If we see a valuable training opportunity, we'll proactively work to take advantage of it. When the training is complete, we announce it to the company. If an employee says, "I'm going to a seminar tomorrow, but it's free, so I'm not going to report it," I tell that person to notify us because we have to document it. Whether it's free or costs $10,000, the point isn't to know how much we're spending; the point is so everyone knows how much we're gaining.

Information about training is e-mailed through the entire company every quarter, and annually, we put a huge poster on the lobby wall. It reads, "Growing our Rockstars" and displays all the things that we did in the past year to grow our team members. The training poster hangs in our lobby because I want every vendor, every potential client, and most importantly, every potential employee to see that we invest in our people.

An annual recap of our team's training and education opportunities are proudly displayed in our lobby so that all visitors (clients, vendors, and potential team members) know how focused we are on growing our team.

A conference seminar is a great way for people to learn new skills, but it's not the only way. Learning is often just as valuable if it's done via a webinar, conference call, or blog. In my opinion, all of those opportunities pale in comparison to the greatest education tool of 'em all. Want to know what it is? (Hint: it's what you're doing right now.)

READING!

Give me a strong cup of coffee and an insightful book, and I'll take that any day over an expensive, remedial seminar. The investment of time and energy demanded by the act of reading makes the lessons learned so much more rewarding, personal, and memorable for the reader. If you have the right book, you're literally carrying a seminar in your pocket. You can refer to it repeatedly. Have you ever read someone's book, liked it, and decided to attend that author's seminar to "learn more"? Then, when you heard the author speak, you were disappointed to learn that the presentation only contained the same info as the book (but less of it)?

That experience plus the belief in the unrivaled educational power of reading books is what led us to create our most-talked-about cultural achievement and our richest investment in our people.

BETTERBOOKCLUB: WE PAY PEOPLE TO READ

Through our specially designed book club, we *pay people to read*. You read that sentence correctly, but let me say it again anyway: we pay people to read. Remember that I said some of this culture stuff is easy and cheap, but some of it is expensive and hard? Well, our book club, officially known as BetterBookClub, is definitely the latter. But let me tell you, it's the best, most effective, and most efficient education we do. It's the most popular cultural initiative we have and the most buzz-worthy thing that people outside our organization talk about. To brag a little more, it's a total home run. And when you see the results through my eyes, you'll agree it's worth every penny we spend and every drop of sweat we shed.

Here's how it all came about. First of all, I'm an avid reader, and I'm constantly acquiring new books to help me grow as a person and a business leader. About seven years ago, my wife pointed at the big stack of business books I'd accumulated at our house and said, "You've got to get these books out of my house." It occurred to me that if I took them to work and made them available there, other people would get good use out of them too. So I brought them to the office, put them on a big shelf, and said, "Anybody who wants to read my books, please read them."

For months, they just sat there. People often are unwilling to pick up an instructional book, because it's kind of a pain in the neck. They did that in school. I admit some of those business, marketing, and management books can look pretty daunting. But I didn't give up. I'd learned some valuable lessons from those books, and I wanted to share them. So, to get people reading books, I used the oldest trick in the book: I paid them. I went back to my team. "Hey, I'm going to go a step further," I said. "I will pay you to read these books. I've written various amounts inside the covers—$25, $50, $75, $100—and if you read the book, I will pay you that much money." That did it. Pretty soon, what started out as a little nudge on my part became a full-blown cultural program that we will never stop doing.

To manage this program, we empowered a champion within our organization to keep up with the books and their use. Then we built an online platform that enabled us to record who'd read what, how much we'd paid them, how they rated the book, who they recommend it to, and a repository for their book reports. The result? Hundreds of participants led to thousands of dollars paid out, tons of knowledge absorbed, lots of insights, many great conversations, and the generation of ideas that led to better things in our company.

I'm continually surprised by the books people enjoy. There are currently over five hundred approved books and videos on the shelves in our foyer, and our library grows by five to ten books a week. We track who reads the most and which books are read most often so that people can create some competition around learning. All the books still have ratings according to their dollar value, and there's a poster in the hall that lists the top twenty books in the company.

When you've paid out as much as we have for reading, sharing the amount,
the team's favorite books, and the most active readers seems like a natural.
Find a way to get books into the the brains of your team.

What's useful about that is if new employees just start by reading the
most popular books, they are immediately on the same page as other
people. At the same time, we don't set limits. If people want to read

a book that no one's read, that's great too. Now they have knowledge and a little insight that, maybe, no one else does. Finally, they don't have to read books for money. Many don't. In our system, people have the ability to tag and report on books outside the pay-to-read program. Hundreds of books have been read that way.

We invest about $10,000 a year and have paid nearly $100,000 over the last seven years to get books into brains. It's an insanely popular program, with a huge participation rate of over 70 percent. We pay and recognize people for taking knowledge from books and applying it to their jobs. The money spent on paying people to read is significant, as are the time and resources used to maintain the system. But the benefits are crazy good.

- **Agile.** Employees who struggle to find quality training in the form of a seminar can *always* target a book that speaks directly to their needs.

- **Effective.** When you invest the time and energy it takes to read (and reread) a book, that information sticks with you in a way that a one-time seminar might not.

- **Efficient.** You could pay a few thousand dollars for an airline ticket, hotel, meals, and per diem for *one* person to attend *one* conference on the clock. Or you could pay the same amount for a hundred people to read hundreds of books on their own time.

Whenever I tell folks about BetterBookClub, they always say, "Well, we'd like to do that. Can we use your system?" The answer used to be no, but by growing the scope and functionality for ourselves, we found a way to share this system with others. At BetterBookClub.com, any company can design and implement its own book club. It doesn't have to be done the way we do it. Certainly, people don't have to be paid to read. In fact, enormous value can be derived from a small collection of ten books if they are the right ten books.

Whatever you do to invest in your employees, just be sure to understand this: innovation or opportunity can come from any place. We all soak up incredible amounts of knowledge if we're open to it. When the student is ready, the teacher appears. I just think that when you're willing to attend training, to absorb information through books, and to respect the opinions of others, big things happen.

By the way, if you are thinking...yeah, we have a book club, consider what I believe to be the top 4 reasons traditional book clubs don't work as intended in organizations:

1. "The boss" tries to shove titles down team members throats.
2. "The boss" says it's important but does not prioritize, recognize, or incentivize.
3. "The boss" does not participate.
4. Growth is not inherently present in the existing culture.

SHARE THE WEALTH

We certainly didn't invent the concept of profit sharing, but we do have a solid perspective on why it works. In the past five years (2009–2015) we have paid out a substantial amount of money—about $1.8 million—in profit-sharing bonuses. It's a really small number if we make $100 million a year. It's a really big number if we make a more reasonable amount. In general, my feeling is that I want to share somewhere between 10 and 20 percent of our profits with the people who do the work. At the end of the year, every team member is eligible for one-tenth of 1 percent of our net profits. So, if Betty Sue has been here one year, she gets one tenth of 1 percent of our net profit. If Betty Sue's been here more than five years, then we double it, and Betty Sue gets two-tenths of 1 percent. If Betty Sue has been here ten years, then Betty Sue gets three-tenths of 1 percent, or three times the basic share. If we were to have a hundred people, we'd give away about 10 percent of our profit.

Every month, we post what our projected annual net profit is going to be and then do the calculation to show employees what their percentage is. If we're going to make $1 million in net profit, the net share per person is $1,000.

If a client leaves the agency, that number may go down, and we may project $700,000 in profit—well, our employees get $700. The next month, we might have some good things happen, and the projected profit might go to $1.2 million. Employees know they're going to get $1,200 at the end of the year. They know that the more they help us make, the more they're going to make. If we were to have a downturn, they'd take a little bit of a hit.

On a micro level, we know that every team member contributes to our bottom line. My question is..."do they?". We believe sharing profits levels and giving each person a fair portion of that profit helps each team member see, feel, and take ownership of their impact.

Profit sharing has been an effective program for us, not only as a way to share but also as a way to communicate the constant ups and downs of the business. The biggest pushback to sharing financial information like this is knowing how to deal with people who are aware of how much the company makes. That's a classic business 101 issue, so I'll give you the classic business 101 answer: most of your employees think you make more than you do, anyway. By sharing that information, all you do is put their world in perspective with yours. It brings team members closer together. By giving them a share of the profits, you give them a share of the voice. You'd better listen to them. Otherwise, why are you giving them a share?

Sharing says, "I believe in you. You can help this company be more successful, and therefore, I'm going to share a piece of the pie with you." The more invested your people are in your corporate success, the more they'll do to ensure it.

INVESTING IN DREAMS

A few years ago, we began one of our most "out-there" cultural endeavors: Dream Manager. Based on the book, *The Dream Manager* by Matthew Kelly, we decided to dive deeper into the concept of investing in our employees. We went beyond professional development and instituted a program in which we help our employees identify and reach their own personal dreams. We were serious about this. We hired a full-time dream manager whose job it was to counsel people through a bucket-list type of process. We made it available to 150 people with the hope of helping them feel more fulfilled in their lives. How, you ask? Here are just a few of the things folks achieved because of the Dream Manager program:

- purchased first home

- renovated a bathroom

- wrote and published a novel

- learned photography

- got a German shepherd

- started an organic food business

Obviously, for some people, it worked. We had people who made some great dreams come true. We even had some people who chased their dreams right out of my shop. Many people still use elements of Dream

Manager to continue the quest to reach their dreams. But in the end, this was not a program that we were able to sustain. People couldn't get past the trust issues of mixing work with their personal lives. Regardless, Dream Manager is definitely something I'm glad we tried, and so are the employees who tried it. Every once in a while, someone comes up to me and thanks me for another dream they checked off their list. Talk about something that was worth getting wrong!

It was kind of crazy, but it was the right thing to do. Investing in people's personal dreams is an idea you should explore.

WHAT IS *EMPLOYEE FRIENDLY?*

Let's start by defining what it isn't. The opposite of employee friendly might be called working for the state. If you work for the state, you probably don't describe your work as employee friendly. You'd probably describe it as a bunch of people who are there because they have to be. As the sales guru Jack Daly says, "You walk into a business, and you can smell the culture." He doesn't mean you can smell what they cooked in the kitchen or what they had for lunch, but you can look at people's faces and you can tell if this is an employee-friendly business or not.

A lot of times, you walk into a retail environment, and you can tell a bunch of "I-don't-cares" are working there. You can walk into a sales culture and tell if it's too cutthroat. In an environment like that, it becomes an *only the strong survive* kind of thing as opposed to an attitude of abundance.

At our place, for all those who come in, we think, *These people came from somewhere, and they're on their way somewhere. What can we do to help them along their way?* If we're not helping our employees to get to a better place than their current job, if we don't look good on our employees' résumés, if people aren't proud to work here, then we've done something wrong. That's no way to go through life. To me, employee friendly means we are as excited about team member growth on every level because we know that team member growth means team growth.

We want people to grow. We want them to get training. We want them to be the best they can be at their jobs. Our employees are expected to find and take advantage of opportunities to grow and expand. Remember when visitors and employees walk into our lobby, the first thing they see is a poster of the company's history of investing in its people. That's by design. If it turns people on, that's great. If it turns people off, they should get the hell out of our lobby.

IF THEY AREN'T MOVING FORWARD, THEY'RE SLIPPING BACK

What would stop you from offering opportunities to your people to get smarter and to be better? Even if it were at your expense, why wouldn't you embrace it? In a word, it's paranoia. If you are thinking, *What if I pay them to read and they leave? What if I pay them to read and they didn't really read the book? What if they're tricking me? What if I sent them to this great training and they meet someone and get a job somewhere else? What if they quit? What if, what if, what if?* Those are all feelings of paranoia. Reject them.

I believe in reverse paranoia, which is the feeling that everything you do is going to create a win for you down the road—*everything*. Everyone is out to help you. Everyone is going to do the right thing first. It will all come back in spades. If you believe that, it's part of building the people around you, as opposed to keeping people down.

We take advantage of growth by letting people take on as much as they can. Our people are offered a lot of opportunities for growth in terms of job responsibility and salary. If your people aren't growing, they're standing still—and so is your company. Can you afford to stand still?

EMPOWER YOUR CHAMPIONS

The biggest mistake that I see all the time happens when the CEO says, "I'll do that." Or the owner says, "I'll take care of that." As an owner, you already have more responsibilities than you can carry. Your people are begging for the opportunity, pleading with you for the chance to manage an area or work a project successfully. Every time you say, "I'll do that. I'll be in charge," you rob them of that opportunity for success.

That's a self induced affliction that all entrepreneurs have and must get over. But they should choose tasks they think no one else but they can do and let others show them how well they can do them. That's how we've been able to sustain programs that I couldn't possibly have sustained on my own.

Every process has to have a champion, a team member who's excited by the program and invested in making it work. There is no program in my company that I'm in charge of that has found success. I may have come back from a conference or a meeting with an idea, but I have no execution skills. That's true of most crazy entrepreneurs. They think they do, but they don't.

Here, everything's run by someone other than me. The morale program is run by someone else. BetterBookClub is run by someone else. The envelope system is run by someone else. The rocker program is run by someone else. Huddles are run by someone else. There's no culture element that I'm directly responsible for. I'm there to make sure that they each have a champion and help them if they get stuck. But I don't even know where the recognition envelopes are. They have made the programs better than I could ever have made them, not just because I can't execute them but also because they're simply too much.

We have a unique niche. We build brands for PI lawyers. We have a team of people who wake up every day and come to work and have one thing to do: build brands for PI lawyers. Some people do that by building websites. Some people do it by producing commercials. Some people improve media schedules, and some people analyze numbers. But they come to work every day and figure out how to make PI lawyers' brands better in their markets.

The champions of our cultural initiatives come to work every day to do their primary jobs, and then they have their champion roles. They're empowered to enlist volunteers, build support teams, and do what they need to do to *champion* the initiative. It's a big responsibility which, for the right person, is its own reward. Give your people the opportunity to grow rather than rob them, and don't put fences around them. When you build fences around your employees, they turn into sheep.

Jack Daly has a great story about the importance of champions. It goes something like this: "We just crossed $100 million in sales. I want everyone to get a $100 bill as a reward. Everybody in the company gets $100 to celebrate our $100 million in sales." He goes to HR and accounting, and he tells the staff in those departments that he wants everybody to get $100. They work on it and get back to him, "Hey, Jack, we've got all this worked out. Everyone's getting $74.23."

He says, "$74.23? What are you talking about? I said $100."

They go, "Yes, but you give them $100, and then after taxes, it comes out to this, and we have to take taxes out. It can't be $100, because blah blah blah…" Boom! They just ruined the program. He insisted, pushed it through, and finally got his employees a $100 bonus.

If I want to give everyone a $1,000 bonus at the end of the year, I could just inform accounting and let it appear in everyone's paychecks. But then, they would only get something like $742.30 added to their normal salaries. It just doesn't have the same "bonus" impact. So how do we correct that? Well, we give that task to a champion and let that person tackle the obstacles in the way. Our champion thinks through the problem and decides to give all the managers bonus envelopes to be handed out the night of our annual holiday party. The card inside the envelope says $1,000. The manager tells his team members, "Hey, this is going to be in your next paycheck, but we wanted you to see that the bonus you're getting is $1,000. Thank you for a great year!" They can say, "Hey, I got a $1000 bonus!" rather than "Hey, after taxes, I got $742.30, and it's getting lumped into my next paycheck two weeks from now."

But now, stop a minute and think about all the steps that are needed to make that happen. Someone's got to make the list. Someone's got to print the cards. Someone's got to make sure that the company logo's on the stuff. Someone's got to stuff the envelopes and pass them out to the team leaders. And then the team leaders can hand out the envelopes and thank their team for a great year's work. It's not easy. Everyone's busy; it's that time of year; we have projects going on. It only happens if a champion empowered by the CEO works to make it happen. Otherwise, it just goes in the paychecks, and no one even notices.

When you find a tactic that is going to improve your culture, give it a champion. Let that person give it KPIs and create reports that you can see regularly. Then find another way to improve your culture, and go through the process again.

MORALE-BUILDING TEAMS:
CHAMPIONS OF CHAMPIONS

One of the best ways to illustrate the importance of empowering a champion is through the example of FiSH!, our employee-run morale-building team. This is an autonomous, employee-driven group, whose mission is to "make work fun." That may sound kind of unimportant, but actually, it's vitally important. Ripped off and duplicated from the book *FiSH!*, this group goes to great lengths to make remarkable things happen at work. It is truly the epicenter of our culture. Armed with a small discretionary budget and the manpower of a few enthusiastic volunteers, this group is responsible for making our work days sparkle with excitement. Beer at desks, milk and cookies at holidays, lunchtime yoga classes, workday parties, free massages, costume contests, Make Your Day gift cards, paper airplane tournaments, company kickball teams, fun employee videos—all this and more falls under their purview. Basically, our FiSH! team has an impact on half the stuff I'm bragging about in this book. I'll bet you can guess why this team functions so well: I empower a champion to oversee it, the FiSH! head.

The FiSH! head's responsibility is awesome in every sense of the word. They plan, coordinate, and help execute everything the group does. We're talking huge projects with huge impacts on our culture. One Valentines Day, FiSH! team members stayed late for several evenings making Valentine cards for the whole staff. These were not the generic, one-size-fits-all, paper-heart Valentine crap you usually see. These were carefully designed Valentine cards that contained handwritten, personalized poems for every single employee in our company. On the morning of Valentine's Day, everyone arrived to find these thoughtful messages waiting for them at their desks. The emotions were all over the place. People laughed, cried, and spent a good bit of the morning sharing their poems with each other. It was a moving experience for new and tenured employees. FiSH! could've done it an easier way. They could've sprinkled a few heart-shaped candies around everyone's desktops, but they didn't. They had a bold vision, made a plan, and executed it.

Of all the things in this book that I hedged on and said, "Meh… it's a good fit for us, but you'll have to find something parallel for you," empowering champions is not one of them. It doesn't matter who you are or how impressive your résumé is. Delegating this kind of authority is a *must*. So, right about now, I would love to share with you the secrets of our morale team's inner workings, such as how often they meet, how they function, how they make decisions, and how they form committees. But I can't, because I have no friggin' idea! My interaction with FiSH! mainly consists of just saying yes a lot. Isn't that a great way to lead? Empower your champions, invest in your employees, and say yes. You'll be glad you did.

HR VS. CULTURE

Chances are, if your company has a Human Resources (HR) person or department, those people are loaded down with more responsibilities than anyone else in the organization. Hiring, firing, promoting, consulting, explaining benefits, enforcing policy, updating manuals, training, and compliance only begin to cover their exhaustive list of tasks. Despite HR already being overworked, underappreciated, and potentially underpaid, many people often associate HR with culture.

With all due respect to the thousands of HR professionals who are doing all they can with all they've got, the myth that HR equals culture is simply not true. You can't lay off the responsibility of building the culture you want on an HR person who's already underwater.

From my perspective…

- HR is not there to create job descriptions. That's your managers' job.

- HR is not there to interview, hire, or even fire people. That's your managers' job.

- HR is not there to review and propel the careers of your team members. That's your managers' job.

- HR is not there to create or run your culture. That's YOUR job.

You're the CEO of your culture, and you need to employ champions outside of HR to help you successfully implement your plans.

Our HR department has only two functions (and it's still a hand full): administer benefits and manage guidelines that keep us out of the courtroom. That's it. Focusing HR allows us to stay lean in this area of our business and invest even more in our cultural programs and champions.

If our team members go to HR for advice on advancing their career, they are redirected to talk to their manager. If they don't think they can talk to their manager, they're advised to go to their director. If they don't think they can talk to their director, they're advised to talk to me, the CEO.

Everyone lumps culture into HR. Don't. HR administrators go to seminars and learn about everything except what you, the CEO, need your culture to be. When you put HR in charge of culture, it potentially becomes a disaster or certainly, not led by design.

Business is hard.
Invest in your team, empower your champions,
and embrace your role as the
CEO of your culture.

CHAPTER FOUR

EMBRACE TOP-DOWN CORE VALUES

So far, it may seem as if everything I've talked about has been employee focused. If you're a CEO or a manager, you may be wondering whether I'm telling you to manage from the bottom up. No! It's the exact opposite.

At John DiJulius's 2014 Secret Service Summit, I saw Rory Vaden, the author of the best seller *Procrastinate on Purpose* and a self-discipline strategist, engage the audience with an interactive exercise that perfectly illustrates the point of this chapter. First, he instructed us to "put our hand in the air." So we all put our hand in the air. Then he said, "Make a circle with your hand by touching your thumb to your forefinger." We did as we were told: we put our hand in the air and touched our thumb to our forefinger. Then he said, "Now, you see that circle you just made with your hand? Put that on your chin." While he was talking, he demonstrated, but instead of putting his hand on his chin, he put it on his cheek. He told us one thing but did something else. Guess what we all did? The entire audience put their hands on their cheeks. He started yelling, "I said 'Put your hand on your chin!'" We all felt stupid, but it wasn't our fault. We got it wrong because he didn't lead by example.

It expresses the point that people follow what their leader does, not what their leaders says. And if leaders don't do the things they say they're going to do, their company is at a disadvantage. Culture reflects leadership.

The good news is there's a really easy way to right the ship. Creating a winning culture starts with some ingredients that every company has but most are getting wrong: core values. If you embrace the right core values, you set your company on the path for success. But core values fail if no one remembers them. They especially fail if management doesn't live by them. Just shouting buzzwords such as *integrity* and *synergy* without following through is like telling people to put their hand on their chin when you put your hand on your cheek. Getting your core values right starts at the top.

THE WRONG WAY

Most of the business books I've read state that every company has its own core values. As a leader, you don't assign those core values; you *discover* them through your people. Sound familiar? For years that's what we did. We followed the textbook process for finding core values: our leadership team wrote down the names of the people in the company who were the best at their jobs. Then we went around the room and reached a consensus on the five people who were really busting their butts for our company and doing a great job.

Next, we asked which words we'd use to describe those people. Everyone wrote down the best attributes of our A-players. The common themes and most frequently repeated words became the text for our core values. That's the process we followed with our ad agency and repeated with two spin-off companies. Three different companies with three different sets of core values, plus my own personal set of four, totaled sixteen different values: four for each of the three companies and four for myself.

Although obviously right, this was also obviously wrong. You can probably guess why. Because there were too many, and I couldn't remember any of them! As I walked from one company to the other, I asked employees to live their work lives according to this list of words that I couldn't recall. Even worse, I couldn't *relate* to them. How could I? I'm not four different people.

I realized that I wouldn't be a good leader if I weren't dead-on in sync with the values of the companies I led. I wouldn't be a good leader if I did not to repeat and demonstrate those values to my staff until they made fun of me and beyond. Something had to change.

I HEAR THAT CHANGE A-COMING

Funny how things work out. Just when we were in a jam, the stars of the universe again aligned to help us. In June of 2013, Nashville's EO Chapter invited author and business coach Larry Linne to share his "Make the Noise Go Away" presentation. Larry was a huge hit. I'd consider his book, his presentation, and his program all "must do" for any entrepreneur. In addition to his presentation to business owners, Larry also offered a ten-month course to help second-in-commands learn to calm the waters and "make the noise go away" for their CEOs. Always fans of learning, our Chief Operating Officer, Chris Stovall, and our Director of Operations, Greg Howell, both felt it would be a worthwhile program.

Working through the program, both came to realize a key misalignment in our organization—a disruption in the force that was creating unnecessary noise and holding back our organization. In what Chris and Greg described as a "light bulb moment," they questioned whether our stated company's core values were out of alignment with my *personal* core values. During a routine check-in meeting, this insight led them to ask me two questions that changed the course of our business forever:

"What specifically are your *personal* core values?" I knew the answer. I had already done the work to identify Confidence, Optimism, Growth, and Respect as the values most important to me. Their second question was more illuminating. They asked, "What would happen if those core values became the company core values?".

MY CORE VALUES

Chris and Greg had already realized, what I and the entire leadership team needed to learn. The core values of the Founder/CEO should be the core values of the company. The Founder/CEO shouldn't be stuttering and stammering his way around these topics. The Founder/CEO should be the Pied Piper or chief cheerleader, confidently and constantly reminding the team of what the company is all about. Do the research yourself, but I believe the most powerful companies are typically those in which the leaders' values are tightly aligned with the companies' values.

As enlightening as this was, we initially feared that these new core values would not initially sound much different to the staff than the four old words they'd be replacing. We had to ask ourselves, "How can we effectively communicate these values to the team in a way that is impactful enough to get their attention, substantial enough to justify the change, and memorable enough to be repeatable?"

The answer became obvious when another leader in our company asked me this: "Arnie, why are these your core values?" Without even thinking about it, I was able to recall distinct stories from my childhood that I believed created and solidified these values. I couldn't (and still can't) tell the stories without my voice cracking and often tears flowing. Hearing how impactful, substantial, and memorable these stories were, we decided on the spot to include them when we told the entire team about the new values and the change that was a-coming.

Here's how it went:

CONFIDENCE

From a very young age, I was fortunate to have a dad who put me in his back pocket and took me with him everywhere he went. So much of what I've learned, who I am, and how I run my business is because of my father. Watching how he interacted with people was the MBA of a lifetime.

When he grew up, he turned the family business into a hardware store where I worked after school when I was growing up. On Saturday mornings, I had to be there at 6:00 a.m., which meant that no matter what I did Friday night, I had to be ready for work at the crack of dawn. Dad used opportunities in the store to teach me business. I learned that when you're at the front of the store, you're in charge—and you'd better be prepared to act like it.

One Saturday morning, when I was about twelve years old, my dad was working in his office in the back of the store and had left me out front to mind the counter. A couple of men came in looking to purchase paint for their weekend house-painting project. I'd been helping stock, mix, and sell paint in the store for a year or two. I had a pretty good idea of what was what, but I was not prepared for the barrage of questions from these patrons—and it showed.

"We're painting our house; what kind of paint should we use?" he asked.

"Uh, well... let me see," I started to reply

"Well, what brands do you sell?"

"Uh, well... uh... we have... uh..."

"How much do you think we need?"

"Uh... I think maybe...."

His questions were gruff and quick, and my answers were weak and slow.

Irritated, the customer finally said, "Son, if you don't know the answers, who does?"

I sheepishly responded, "Well, my daddy's in the back."

To which he glaringly responded, "Son, maybe you need to go get your daddy."

Never before and never since have I felt so small. With my tail between my legs, I went back to get my father. When he came out, he was instantly able to engage the men. He confidently led with, "Let me tell you what I've seen other people do." He told him about the paint they'd used, how much they used, and how that had worked out. He jumped right in with total confidence. It was beautiful.

I've never forgotten that moment, and since then, I've always done my best to speak with that same confidence. Whether I am 100 percent sure or not, I want to project confidence and give others confidence. "Go get your daddy" is something I didn't ever want to hear again, and I don't want you all to hear it either. In our work here, I always want you to project confidence.

My family heritage is Syrian/Lebanese. As an Arab in small-town Arkansas in the late 1930s, my dad was called names: "dago," "wop," and other slurs that actually fit his heritage! He was a fighter and a bull of a man. When he was called names or saw others being put down, he'd fight. But he raised me to handle things the smart way, not the physical way. He always preached the same thing: "Get an education. Learn,

GROWTH

learn, learn. Knowledge will set you free from ignorance and from the ignorant."

My father went to the school of hard knocks, but he wanted better for his son. He was proud that I was the first in my immediate family to graduate from college and meet his challenge to "get an education." To this day, I follow his advice. I read books incessantly. I read the labels on cans. I watch documentaries. I want to know more than the average bear. I see that as being willing to grow, not settling for the status quo. I've always believed in growth and the potential of others. I want you to challenge yourself to know more, become a better person, and *embrace growth* whenever it presents itself within this organization.

RESPECT

Even before I was working at the store, when I was five or so, Dad would stick me in the truck with him to get supplies for the hardware store. We would go to Little Rock or Memphis, which were both about an hour away. I learned to drive sitting in his lap. I'd slide across the front seat, and he'd let me steer the truck. It was awesome. He taught me the capital of every state in the country, and he taught me the name of every river we crossed. I learned to read from road signs, and he'd quiz me about what they said. Pulling a trailer behind us, we'd make stops at the paint wholesaler, the lumber wholesaler, the door-frame guy, or the general hardware supplier. Along the way, we'd load up until the truck and trailer were full. I was Dad's little man, and I went on all the trips.

In every place I walked into, I'd meet the dockworker, the sales guy, and if possible, I'd go in and meet the vice president or the president of the company. My dad would always introduce me as though I were an adult. He taught me to shake their hands, look them in the eye, and tell them I appreciated them letting me come in. Sometimes, I'd get a gumball or a sucker, a little reward for my effort, and I thought that was the coolest thing in the world. That's how I learned that you had to be nice all the way in the door, not just in the back office. You're nice to the second guy, the third guy, and the fourth guy. Then you get a gumball!

But as all of us do, I became a teenager and started forgetting some of the lessons. One Sunday afternoon, I was sitting in a recliner in my house, watching football. My uncle Isaac, my dad's brother, arrived. Uncle Isaac was a classic statesman. Over the years, he had taught me how to play pool, respect religion, and appreciate family. Uncle Isaac was a man among men. He said, "Hello, Arnie." I gave him the ol' teenage "Hey." Didn't even look up; just went, "Hey."

He immediately turned to my dad and said, "That's how your son greets his elders? That's what I can expect when I come into your house?" *Ouch.* My dad was devastated, and so was I, for having embarrassed him. I'd made him look like a bad parent because I didn't have the courtesy to get up and say hello to his elder brother, which of course was the right thing to do. I've never forgotten that moment. Nor did I ever fail to get up and properly greet my uncle, or anyone, again.

Respect can't be a sometimes quality; respect is an always quality, and when you respect the people around you, good things tend to happen. When it comes to your clients, visitors, coworkers, vendors, yourself, I implore you to *respect everyone.* That's how we're gonna conduct business in this company.

OPTIMISM

My dad taught me to be optimistic. There are always two ways to look at a negative event: "The sky is falling!" or "Look at this cool stuff coming out of the sky." I've always had the ability to frame up stories just a little bit better. You can call it embellishment, and you can call it wishful thinking, but to me, it's seeing a story with the best possible outcome. My life hasn't been without challenges and tragedy. My sister ran away from home when I was in second grade. It was an incredibly tough time for our family. One morning, my teacher asked me, "Have they found your sister yet?" The truth was I didn't know what was going on. But the only way I knew to cope was to hope for the best. I replied, "I think she's with friends. I think she's gonna be okay, and we can't wait to see her." It was an optimistic approach to an otherwise unsettling situation. Later, when I was ten, tragedy struck our family again. My older brother died in a terrible accident. As you would expect, it was an excruciating loss for me and my family. But determined to move forward, I always talked about it in terms of what he had done for me while I was growing up, rather than in terms of the pain I felt. These events have shaped my optimistic view of life. If someone else could go to college, I could go to college. If someone else could make it in a sport, I could make it in a sport. I may have been the world's worst baseball player (my friends told me so, anyway), but I optimistically put in the effort and played.

I bring that optimism to my business. One of my many favorite sayings is one I learned as a parent: *no* means *maybe*, and *maybe* means *yes*. You just need to drive toward *yes*. I believe that. I believe that I can talk anybody into anything if it's the right thing to do. I go back to the fact that my dad was a salesman. He built houses, ran a store, and did a lot of other things, but at the end of the day, he sold for a living—and he always got to *yes*. The difference between a huckster and a salesman, in my opinion, is that the huckster gets to *yes* no matter what. I drive toward *yes* when I know it's the right thing to do. As in life, obstacles will always be a part of business. *Choose optimism*, and overcoming them will be easier.

That's how I rolled out our core values: personal stories that represent the guiding principles of my life. Now we have values that I believe in and my staff members completely understand. Going forward, when our team thinks about *project confidence*, they're reminded of the get-your-daddy story. Or when they recognize a fellow employee for demonstrating our core value of respecting everyone, they're reminded of my uncle Isaac and how important respect is in business and in life. Our core values are personal to me. The stories behind them make them memorable to everybody else.

There's also a practical reason for codifying top-down core values. Even in world-class companies, the leaders, managers, and workforce change a lot more than the owner does. For example, we came up with our first set of core values in 2005. Other than me, just two members of that first ten-member executive team were still with the company in 2015. Every year, life happens, people leave, and the team changes. Are we going to revise the values every year to reflect that? No, it's just not feasible or effective. I, however, am a constant, and in your business, you are a constant. Make sure your core values are as well.

Embracing top-down core values is your chance to make your mark as a leader. They're the foundation for your culture, which is the catalyst for your execution. Obviously, different companies grow from different beginnings. Maybe you're not the sole proprietor of a small company, as I am. Maybe you're a leader at a large corporation or a manager of a large department. Whatever your circumstance, there's a story somewhere that will make your values ring louder. If you're skeptical about following my philosophy, all I can say is this: If you don't believe in your core values, who the hell will? Dig deep for the story people can understand and remember. Pour your heart into it, and the right culture will follow.

SIMPLE BUT HARD EXERCISE FOR DISCOVERING YOUR CORE VALUES

We all believe what we believe for a reason. Ask yourself what you think your core values are. Then ask yourself why. If the stories flow easily, those are your core values.

Business is hard.
Leading with your core values
will make it easier.

CHAPTER FIVE

GENERATE UNAVOIDABLE CULTURE (GO BIG!)

AVERAGE IS THE NEW SHITTY

Let me just come out and say it: average sucks. Being an average place to work is even worse than being a terrible place to work, or as your disgruntled employees like to say, a "shitty" place to work. Why? Because people don't put up with shitty. They leave. *Average*, however, creates a quandary for people. They wonder whether, if they leave their *average* place, they'll wind up at a *shitty* place. So they stay. In other words, *average* is the worst culture most people will tolerate for an extended period of time. Don't subject yourself or your staff to average.

People spend a lot of time at work. Their home away from home should be a rewarding, energizing, safe, and comfortable place to spend over forty hours a week. The culture you design needs to be planned well enough to be respectful but dramatic enough to be unavoidable. Don't think in watered-down, pastel colors. Think in *loud, bright, and bold* colors. Go big or go home! Let's explore what I mean by "unavoidable" culture.

Everyone is having a jolly ole time as we celebrate Christmas in July in costume, complete with camels delivering cookies and tidings of joy. Yes, that's my partner Jimmy, our COO Chris, and me dressed as Elf 1, Elf 2, and Santa respectively. Big events are unavoidable.

THE HOSPITALITY TRICK

There's a secret trick for making people feel truly welcome. Folks in the service or hospitality industries already know it. (It's great for cocktail parties too!) Now I'm sharing this trick with you. When people come to your office or any place where you're the host, you may want to make them feel welcome and relaxed by offering them a beverage. Sounds simple, but there's a right and wrong way to do it. Here's the wrong way:

"May I get you something to drink before the start of the meeting?"

Now here's the unavoidable way:

"At this meeting, we're serving coffee and sparkling water. Which will you have?"

Why was the *wrong way* wrong? Because people may decline for fear they're imposing. That's no fun! Why was the *unavoidable way* unavoidable? Obviously because declining wasn't an option. Now everybody's on the same page! Here's how we use this nice touch of hospitality to spark unavoidable culture in our business.

We had a Christmas-themed day at work. What's so big about that? Well, as I write this, it's July in Tennessee, which means a week ago, it was a zillion degrees outside and humid, not exactly your traditional Christmas weather. Nevertheless, we invited people to arrive in whatever holiday garb they deemed appropriate for the theme of Christmas in July. We knew it was kind of a weird, confusing concept, and many might opt out of it. So our morale team requested that my business partner and I do something to jump-start this new, quirky cultural event. Per their wishes, we dressed up in white beards, Santa hats, and incongruous beachwear: Hawaiian shirts, sandals, and shorts. At 7:30 a.m. we hid just inside the main employee entrance. As folks trickled in, we jumped out at them and yelled "Ho Ho Ho!" and gave them all a hug. Then we demanded that they all have their picture taken with us in our ridiculous outfits before proceeding to their desks. You could not get by us without having this damn picture taken. We were, literally, ambushing our staff with culture, and it was awesome. For nearly two hours, we turned every morning-commute scowl into a broad smile of surprise. Sounds cute, right? We were just getting started.

True to the spirit of our staff, many people arrived in their own Christmas-in-July getups, but for the people who forgot or chose not to dress up, we had Hawaiian leis and little stockings with candy waiting on their desks. In our break room, a hearty breakfast was ready for everyone in our building. Later in the afternoon, the morale team pushed a food cart with milk and Christmas cookies around to every desk and gave away prizes for best attire. The whole affair was pretty corny, but it provided a much-needed morale boost during the doldrums of summer. Events like this are what I mean by *unavoidable culture*.

Our work calendar is brimming with special theme-oriented events and perks that are designed to make work fun. We do tailgates in the parking lot for the start of football season and timely intra-office competitions that jive with current events such as the Olympics or World Cup. We have folks that organize the typical stuff, such as softball, kickball, and fantasy football leagues. And when there's nothing else going on, we go with our ol' standby of beer camels, baby! On random Fridays, members of our morale team dress up in camel costumes and push around a mail cart packed with assorted beverages and ice. They stop by every desk and hand out twelve-ounce bottles of gratitude that simply convey the message of "Hey, thanks for a week of good work. Beer's on us!" A lot of companies wouldn't even dream of allowing light drinking at work. But we trust our folks to have a good time once in a while. All our employees love the beer camels. How could they not? Beer camels are unavoidably fun.

Here are a few of my other favorite events that illustrate what unavoidable culture is all about.

- **Halloween decoration contest.** Departments hold a contest to see who can decorate their work areas the best. Participation is so intense that our entire building ends up looking like a haunted house. Everyone is dressed up. Every nook and cranny is tricked out with scary decor. The staff is so gung ho you'd think the winning department was getting an extra week's vacation. But actually, the prize (a pizza party) is superfluous. The real prize is the fun of doing it and the pride in doing it well.

- **Jimmy's Holiday Party.** Jimmy Bewley is my business partner and cofounder of our ad agency. He's responsible for an innumerable amount of creative and strategic accomplishments. Perhaps his greatest (and certainly most popular) contribution to our success is his coordination of our annual holiday party, aptly named Jimmy's Holiday Party. Highlights include an open bar, DJ, bonus announcement, employees of the year recognition, and best of all, lavish door prizes, which are completely paid for by company-earned American Express points. The enthusiasm and turnout for this event is as strong as any business can hope for in a holiday party.

- **cj Conference.** Once a year, we invite all of our clients and key collaborators to come to our town and powwow with us. For two days, we're learning, exchanging ideas, interfacing, showcasing work, building trust, strengthening relationships, and having fun. This truly is where our culture and business perfectly align.

- **Thanksgiving.** Much as they do for Christmas in July, members of our team, including leadership, dress up like turkeys and pilgrims and jump out at people as they show up for work. There's a catered breakfast, pictures with the pilgrims, and a host of seasonal décor to give folks a taste of Thanksgiving before the holiday break.

- **Stay-cation.** A brilliant concept hatched by our morale team, stay-cation is another attempt to beat back the summertime blues. Lots of people take vacation in the summer. For those still at work, the office feels kind of desolate and lonely. Stay-cation is a week-long event filled with vacation-like happenings: summer attire, beach games, food trucks in the parking lot, competitions, beer camels, and tons of fun.

CONSTANT CULTURE: WEAR IT ON YOUR SLEEVE

Culture doesn't have to take the form of big tent-pole events. In fact, unavoidable culture can have more impact if it's deeply woven into the fabric of your day-to-day routine. One of the best examples I can think of is our dress code. Basically, we don't have one. At cj, we're a casual-dress office. It's comfortable, fun, and ridiculously easy to manage. Remember how daunting our BetterBookClub might have seemed? Our dress code is the opposite. Here's the step-by-step process to fully implement a casual dress code:

Step 1: Tell your staff that dress is casual.

Step 2: That's it.

Once you say you're going casual, you'll never have to say it twice! Maybe set a few decency guidelines and bam! The flip-flop parade will be marching through your door. The cultural impact is massive on all fronts. Internally, your people are comfortable and happy. Externally, visitors can get an instant read on your culture upon their first visit. Our clients really dig it. They know that when they come to our house, they can relax and let their hair down. On the days when we're hosting or visiting an event at which we're outwardly representing the company, we spiffy up with company-branded shirts and sweaters. The staff doesn't mind dressing up a bit, because they can wear whatever they want the other 360-ish days of the year.

If casual dress is something you can and want to do, then just do it! In spite of its name and easy implementation, a casual dress code is an example of culture that is brash, bold, and unavoidable. It also illustrates one of my favorite axioms: "Don't make rules for the masses based on the sins of a few." Why? Because rules suck the life out of culture. One rule becomes two. Two rules become three. Pretty soon you've got a handbook that's a list of don'ts. Try to make your handbook a list of dos. Sounds scary? It doesn't have to be. Just be consistent, and your culture will find a way to police itself. Don't tell people what to wear. If you like to see your staff rocking company gear, give them a variety of comfortable, stylish options. We give away all kinds of stuff with our logo on it: fleeces, T-shirts, sweaters, mugs, and hats. A few times a year, people are *asked* to wear their company gear. The rest of the time, people regularly wear company stuff, which I must confess I love.

If you work in a more formal business environment where suits are mandatory, find a way to turn that into a positive thing. Bring in a tailor once a month to do free alterations. Provide discounted dry cleaning, or better yet, make it free. Challenge another firm to a best-dressed competition. Just make sure cultural decisions like this are intentional.

MAKE FAMILIES FEEL WELCOME

Being dog and kid friendly is among the bolder aspects of cj's every-day-culture vibe. Why do I lump kids and dogs together? Because we love 'em both equally, and our guidelines for both initiatives are hilariously similar.

From cj Advertising's *Employee Handbook*:

DOG FRIENDLY	KID FRIENDLY
cj loves dogs!	If team members' kids occasionally need to come to the office, cj welcomes them.
Team members from cj are encouraged to bring their dogs to work on occasion. Owners are encouraged to use good judgment when bringing dogs to work. Please observe the following guidelines when doing so:	Parents are asked to use good judgment when bringing their kids to work. Please observe the following guidelines when doing so:
1. Check your dog in at the front desk.	1. Check your child in at the front desk.
2. Keep your dog either on a leash or with you at all times.	2. Keep your child either on a leash or with you at all times.
3. Avoid forcing coworkers to interact with your dog.	3. Avoid forcing your coworkers to interact with your child.
Make sure your dog is not disruptive of the work environment. If your dog becomes agitated, have an exit strategy. At cj, we reserve the right to ask team members to take their dog home if it disrupts the work environment.	Make sure your child is not disruptive of the work environment, and if your child becomes disruptive, please have an exit strategy. cj reserves the right to ask team members to take their children home when they disrupt the work environment.

Notice how those guidelines have few requirements? Our culture has attracted folks who simply "get it." They understand that our ad agency is not a day-care center. You can't bring your kids here every day of the summer or holiday break. But let's face it. Conflicts happen. There are school cancellations and holidays that don't line up. Sometimes, finding child care becomes a full day's work. Nobody wants that. In those tough, occasional instances, just bring your child in. We've got some toys, a Wii in the break room, and cool people who understand what you're going through. We've had managers bouncing their babies on their knees during meetings. We've had dogs snoring under desks during conference calls. Somehow, we all managed to survive. Actually no, that's not true. We're not surviving; we're thriving. Our culture, our morale, and our product is *better* because we welcome kids and dogs to occasionally come to work. Some business owners say, "I could never do that." You can. You just choose not to. But if that's your choice, consider these other alternatives that celebrate those near and dear to your employees:

1. A photo wall for employees' pets: we do this.

2. A photo wall for employees' kids: we do this.

3. Birthday gift cards for kids and spouses: we do this.

4. Designated kid days at special times of the year such as Halloween or Christmas: we *should* do this.

5. A dog show in the parking lot: I need to write this down. We should *totally* do this!

OTHER EVERYDAY STUFF WITH BIG IMPACT

Your people should feel safe, comfortable, and respected the moment they arrive at work. That's why we make sure that our facilities rock. I'm not trying to brag, but for us, our facilities and the team that maintains them are terrific. Our break room has natural light, plenty of microwaves, filtered water, two ice machines (one of them Sonic ice), ample storage and fridge space, Starbucks coffee, extensive vending options for snacks and meals. The decor is modern and very inviting. Our bathrooms are clean and pleasant. Our parking situation is well thought out and convenient. We're always trying to improve, but I'm pretty happy with where we are. Your facilities should rock also.

Another way to show people you respect them is by being considerate of their time by running efficient meetings and insisting on punctuality. One of the most respectful "everyday" things we do is quiet time. From 1:00 p.m. to 2:00 p.m., everyone's calendars are busy. Busy with what, might you ask? None of your business; that's quiet time, a daily meeting-free hour that is reserved for everyone to get stuff done. Even on days that are chock-full of meetings, people at least have a sacred hour to think and work. Any business can do this. Many do. Why don't you?

COMMUNICATION: GET RID OF BUSINESS JARGON

I'm sure you've probably been reprimanded by consultants and advised by executive coaches to loosen up your lingo. As someone who's guilty of overusing *synergy* as a catchall word and *leverage* as a verb, let me just say this: they're right. Business jargon is a culture killer. Stop sounding like an automated press release. You're a real human. Talk as a human talks. Better yet, write as a human writes. Your e-mails, your texts, your speeches, your voice messages, and yes, even your press releases need to be written in a conversational way. Every time you use jargon such as "We're well positioned," an angel loses its wings. If you want a glossary of business terms to avoid, just look at any mutual fund's prospectus and avoid using those words. If needed, do some R&D, using our employee handbook. The style is professional yet conversational. Want to hear how our culture sounds, call our main line at 615.254.6634 and see if this attracts or repels you.

NAME THAT CULTURE!

You want to talk about unavoidable culture. Give your culture a name. Better yet, give it a name and then give it a mascot. Your company is a team. Teams have nicknames and mascots, iconic symbols around which the team can rally. Maybe this is the ad exec in me talking, but I believe that anything worth doing is worth branding. Branding breathes life into any endeavor. At cj, our culture is called Camel Culture, and our mascot is a camel. We have camels all over our building. Some are hidden, like Mickey at Disney World. Others are big and in your face on posters, videos, and newsletters. And some are employees wearing camel costumes. The camel represents *our* story. Your job is to find *your* story and find a catchy, branded way to remind people of it.

When I preach to audiences, I say, "You don't have to do anything I'm doing, but you've got to do something that makes it your own." If you call your culture Camel Culture, it will fail (unless you too happen to be an Arab redneck). It's got to jive with who you are. As the owner, you *are* the business. I don't mean you have to be there every minute or make over your people in your image, but who you are definitely dictates how your culture works. That's why it's important that the person in the mirror is someone worth following when you're trying to create an employee-friendly workplace.

Examine your weekly routine and search for ways to make your culture unavoidable. Remember to go big or go home!

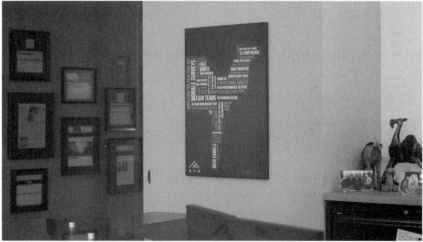

Our mascot is a camel. Every part of our culture that makes us unique is displayed inside this camel, and this poster is displayed throughout our office including our main lobby.

**Business is hard,
but an unavoidable culture is the fun part!**

CHAPTER SIX

HIRE FOR CULTURE

MY TWO GREATEST MISTAKES: BAD HIRING

You've probably figured out by now that culture is people. So it follows that nothing is more vital to your culture (and your success) than whom you hire and how you hire them. It's your primary responsibility to create a culture that attracts the right people. It doesn't matter if your business is the coolest of the cool. Unless you hire great people and treat them well, other great people are not going to beat a path to your door. In business, you're always building the bike while you ride it. You're building your culture *while* you're making the widgets *while* you're hiring people. None of these tasks can take a backseat to the others.

If you accept that culture is king (as I do), then your hiring practices should reflect the philosophy of putting culture first, with a willingness to get it wrong on your way to getting it right. In fact, hiring mistakes constitute the two hardest corporate culture lessons I ever had to learn. I'm about to share two painful examples of personnel decisions that I made and that had a negative impact on our culture, crippled client relationships, and hampered the bottom line. I now refer to them as the expert story and the whatever story. Please learn from them.

THE EXPERT STORY

Success breeds success. After several years of growing brands in the legal business, we learned that our clients had an important business need that could be better served through outsourcing: inbound calls. Entrepreneurially speaking, this revelation definitely got our attention! In response, we launched Legal Intake Professionals (LIP), a 24/7 inbound call center for law firms. For us, forming LIP was an ambitious spin-off venture. We didn't know much—squat, in fact—about the inbound call business, but our most trusted clients assured us that the demand for this service was quite real. After taking the initial plunge, we were able to tread water for a few years. But as many start-ups soon realize, our inexperience was a burden too great to bear. We were sinking. It seemed pretty obvious that we needed a lifeline to someone with the experience and knowledge we lacked. We needed an expert, and I was determined to hire one—we'll call him Jake. Jake was a consultant with tons of pertinent experience. Just glancing at his résumé, I thought he appeared to be a slam dunk who could take us in a new direction. He did just that. But because I made that hire with complete disregard for our culture, that new direction was down.

Soon after arriving, Jake started making operational changes to align our business with the best of the best. But he also started to affect the culture in ways that were anything but the best. When I asked Jake about his decisions, he convinced me I had nothing to worry about, but his actions continued to consistently undercut my beliefs and our culture. For a year and a half, Jake worked behind my back, circumventing my leadership philosophy. First, he cut too many different deals with various clients. That blew up. Our organization is built on a culture of transparency. We want our clients to learn as much from each other as they do from us. The only way they can learn is by talking openly and honestly, which includes sharing sensitive information such as *quoted prices from our call center!* The inconsistent pricing caused tempers to flare and trust to plummet. That was bad enough, but how he treated our team members was equally detrimental. He referred to the intake specialists as "cattle" that can be "herded and replaced."

Basically, he was just a numbers guy. He narrowed everything down to time, rates, and volume. He had little consideration for quality, skill, or compassion. Let me pause to remind you that taking inbound calls for injury lawyers means talking to accident victims who've been seriously injured. Frequently, these calls involve family fatalities. Compassion, skill, and quality really are *the* most important ingredients.

Jake didn't see it that way. His whole attitude was about cracking the whip, pushing down the costs, increasing efficiency, and raising prices. He would say, "It's all about the time on the phone, how much money you're making, how much money you're spending." He wanted to run the company by the numbers, not by the people.

We realized that Jake epitomized the standard industry shortcomings we were trying to outperform and outclass. Literally, he nearly brought us to bankruptcy. How was that worth doing wrong? Because the consequences really got us off our asses. He took us so far down a nasty trail that it spring-boarded us into the most productive opportunity of the company's future. I don't know that we could have gotten there if he hadn't taken us to this really bad place.

It was an embarrassing moment for me. Instead of going with my gut, I went with his plan. We still have people here who worked under Jake, and I still feel guilty that I subjected them to that terrible culture of feeling disrespected, unworthy, and small.

I am also still a little angry at where this person took us, but I'm thankful that we never stopped moving forward. His negative impact became the propellant that pushed us toward success and gave us complete clarity about how to run this business. Now, we have one and only one pricing plan, which has restored the trust of our clients. We constantly respect, honor, and recognize our team members as the awesome people they are. Now that we've refocused our energy to make sure that they have a positive work environment, our metrics, numbers, financials, and client satisfaction ratings are all up. Imagine that!

To his credit, we will never forget Jake.

THE WHATEVER STORY

The second big embarrassment of my working life is what I call the whatever story. *Whatever* is a word that I do not allow in my home. My kids can't say it. My wife—well, she can say anything she wants, but I prefer she not use the *whatever* word. One of my core values is *respect*, and to me, *whatever* is a profoundly disrespectful, dismissive, and insolent word. My family knows that. When they're mad at me, they'll throw out the *whatever*, and that's one of the worst things you can say to me. It's like a four-letter word in my mind.

We once had a department manager with whom I was at odds over the direction she was taking. It's clear to me, now more than ever, that our values weren't aligned. The resulting friction was painful for everyone. One day, my wife came to the office for lunch. This particular department head was at our table, along with some other coworkers. As it happens, this conversation, which probably should have stayed on lighter topics, went off in a business direction. I asked the department head a question about her department's progress. The answer was not the answer I had anticipated, so I said, "I just don't think that's the right direction. We need to do X, Y, and Z, and this is the reason why."

Her response was a venomous, "Whatever."

My wife literally gasped out loud. She knew that had we been at home rather than at the office, my head would have exploded. Because I was in a public, professional setting, I chose to let it go. I should have fired her on the spot, or at least that week, not because of that single remark but because of all the incidents during her time with our company that had embodied her *whatever* attitude. This moment simply confirmed that she had no respect for what our organization was trying to get done.

But I didn't fire her. It was too convenient to leave her in place. It was too convenient to let her continue to take her department in a direction I suspected it shouldn't go but didn't have time to deal with. That lead me to pain and embarrassment because she didn't treat our people or our clients in the way they should have been treated. Eventually, we did part ways but not before her actions had caused internal and external damage to our organization, damage we are *still* working to undo. That experience became my number-two greatest embarrassment. Even writing about it, I cringe. In fact, at the office we refer to her as Voldemort—a.k.a. She Who Must Not Be Named—because of her negative impact on our culture.

Both of these experiences were devastating and humbling and brought me close to disaster, but if you were to ask me, "Arnie, are you glad those things happened?" My answer would always be yes. If they hadn't happened, I wouldn't have learned the lessons I learned. I wouldn't have felt the pain, I wouldn't have grown, and I wouldn't have stretched.

There's an old English ritual known as beating the bounds, in which boys were taken to the boundaries of their parish and beaten. The purpose was to make them remember, and thus defend, their parish's property. Not a very politically correct practice, but the point is the same: pain creates indelible memories that cannot be erased. I'm thankful for these and the thousands of other mistakes that I've made and that caused me pain and taught me lessons I'll never forget.

I don't tell these stories to say, "Look at me." I tell these stories to say, "Look at you." Look inward and find the stories that make you who you are. Find the painful moments that you most vividly remember but don't want to repeat.

ATTRACT THE BEST

Ever since that guy told me he didn't want my company on his résumé, my goal has been to create a company that would look strong on anyone's résumé. We had to become a place with the culture, communication, and values that would attract the attention and respect of others.

So we're pretty vocal about what we have going here to get the world to recognize the unique things we're doing. At times, it feels as if we've become our own little cheering section. We apply for awards and host entrepreneurial events. We make a lot of videos that poke fun at ourselves to show that we have a culture in which "wrong" is okay. It may just seem like a little self-hype, but for us, it's a necessity. We're working against a public bias. In some people's minds, we don't work for "glamorous" accounts. We work for PI lawyers. We have to be proactive to overcome what might be perceived as our handicap. Our goal is to create stories for people to talk about. What may be a survival tool for us can easily be an advantage for you.

Here's an idea: make sure the good things in your company are being leveraged and are being recognized via awards. Begin by assembling a list of all the possible accolades a company can earn: best of this, best of that, best places to work, best in business, best in show, and so on. Then strategically choose the ones you feel are worth your time.

Assign someone to be a champion for this cause. Have them be responsible to fill out the inevitable applications and keep up with the fact sheets and bios you'll need to supply. Task them with communicating why your company is a great place to work and why you're the best in the business. Have a media kit ready to send to anyone who requests information about your company. That develops efficiency around marketing yourself. It's also important to show up for the awards you win because, as Yogi Berra said, "Showing up is 90 percent of the game." Don't do too many, because the market will get sick of you. Do the right ones and do them consistently.

Use your website intelligently to attract talent. I'm always amazed at how people let this slide and miss an opportunity. Use your social media presence to talk about your people and your culture and all the great things you've got going on. Our social media for cj Advertising and LIP is packed with blurbs, videos, and pictures illustrating how we make work fun, recognize success, and inspire visitors to tell us they wish their workplace were more like that. Everything you do should be a beacon to talent. If it's not, you could be repelling future A-players without ever getting to meet them.

IF YOU CAN'T ATTRACT 'EM, GET 'EM

Our number-one source of new hires is referrals. That should tell you something important about our culture. People like it here so much that they're eager to bring their friends on board. We reward these referrals with money based on how long the employee stays. For every job posted, we put a bounty that can be worth anywhere from $1,000 to $10,000 or, conceivably, more. Say the position we're hiring for has a $4,000 bounty. If you refer the person who takes that job, we'll pay you $4,000, incrementally, over a year. This policy is a winning one for everyone involved. Referral hires tend to stay longer, and the referring employees are truly invested in the new hire's success.

Let me be clear. It's not always hugs and kisses around here. Clients get mad, mistakes get made, there's yelling, there's tension, shit happens. You can't avoid these things in the workplace any more than you can in your family. If you're going to experience those things anyway, why wouldn't you do it surrounded by people you like? We have found that most productivity comes out of people who like working together. What a concept!

HIRE FOR CULTURE, EDUCATE FOR SKILL

I love top talent. Everyone does. It's easy to say we want to hire top talent, but I want something more than that. I want people who are willing to grow, learn, and be a part of a team. The talent will come if you spend time doing the work. I don't need everyone to be an A-player in terms of experience; I need A-players in terms of attitude.

Even in sports, culture eats execution for lunch. It's terribly rare that pulling together a bunch of all-stars makes for a championship team. Why? Because they're a bunch of all-stars, not a team. There's no chemistry, there's no heart, there's no culture.

My position is to hire for culture and educate for skill. I know a million people have said that, but it's true. My most abominable business failures didn't happen because our people weren't talented;

they happened because the people involved didn't have their hearts in tune with our company.

Culture happens in every company, but if it's without purpose, without a guiding set of principles, then it's usually not one you want to display. We purposely post things that reflect who we are. We post people getting their recognition envelopes at the staff meeting. We post pictures of us having a great time at our holiday party. We post pictures of ourselves interacting with clients. We post dressing up like a turkey on Thanksgiving Day, and we post pictures of ourselves eating together and giving cards to each other on Valentine's Day. Others see what we do, what we look like, and how we act. You're either repelled or attracted, but there are no surprises about our culture.

MAKING THE CUT

So you've put the word out about the open position you're looking to fill, and you've got a stream of people lined up at your door. How do you figure out which of them will be the best possible fit for the job and the workplace?

Here's the typical hiring process: Most companies start by going over the applicants' résumés for their skills and background, and then they choose the people they want to talk to on the phone about the job. Once they've talked to the applicants on the phone, they bring them in for an interview. They'll let the applicant meet with two or three people in the company, and then they'll make a hiring decision.

That's not how we do it.

After we collect a bunch of applications, I tell my people, "You have twenty seconds to look at every résumé and no more. In that time, you either reject it outright because the applicant's clearly not qualified, or we default to yes, and they move on through the process."

Either the applicants have a general background that matches what we're looking for, or they don't. That should be clear very quickly.

The next step is a series of group interviews, with groups of up to eight prospects in each batch. Once we get eight people in a room, we sit them down and ask a few easy, ice-breaker questions that anyone can answer: "Tell me about the town you grew up in," or "What's the last book you read; would you recommend it to others, and why?" Then every person, in sixty seconds or less, answers the same question all the way around the table. Starting with a different person each time, you repeat this process but with questions that get increasingly more specific to the role you're attempting to fill. "Rank roles in order of comfort, most to least: team member, team leader, or working independently," or "What was the most rewarding creative project you ever worked on?"

Sometimes, the pressure is on the people who answer first because they don't have time to contemplate an answer. Other questions with only either/or answers are designed to put pressure on those who speak last because they may feel the need to answer in a more original way. At the end of this procedure, you will know the two or three people who fit your culture. Those are the ones whom you invite back for another interview.

What are we looking for in their answers? We're looking for our core values, in their words, their body language, and how they react to other people. We're looking for people who can express themselves and have values that we share. People who say, "I grew up in a small town, but I always wanted to grow out of the town," could mean they have a growth mind-set. We're looking for personality and how respectful applicants are when someone else is talking. As a measure of their optimism, we're looking at how they believe they will develop and grow and how confident they are in their opinions and presentation. What you look for is up to you.

After that, we bring back the two or three applicants who appeared to be the right fit. These finalists will have one-on-one interviews with the hiring manager to talk about their actual skills. We know that we have a potential culture fit, so now we're going to dive deeper. If they get through that interview, they're invited to come back for a realistic job preview. They'll spend a half day or full day with the team they would work with, and they'll do some of the actual work they would do if hired.

Finalists who get through all of that take a personality test, which helps us determine if the person we're seeing is really in there. We don't use it as an absolute; it's just there to provide a confirmation of our decision. If we have three strong candidates, it can help us sort them out and rank them.

So, to recap:

- Group interview unearths solid cultural fits.

- First individual interview verifies the needed skills are in place.

- Realistic job preview determines if a finalist is a fit with the team.

- Personality test confirms all.

Does this sound exhaustive and time consuming? If so, I would challenge any company to compare its process to ours. Does your process look something like this? Collect forty résumés, conduct multiple phone interviews, one-on-ones, and follow-ups. Host a staggered finalist round where the candidates dazzle you: they take their meds, get dressed up, and put on a show. How many people do they have to meet one-on-one? How many weeks go by to find the right fit? Add up the time that you're spending on filling a position, and compare your timeline to mine. The fact is that we're doing our process in half your time, and we're getting more accomplished.

HIRING AT THE EXECUTIVE LEVEL

Some people I've talked to are concerned about our way of hiring. They believe it's effective for desk-level jobs, but they wonder how far up the chain it will work. The problem with hiring for executive-level jobs is that you're not going to get this huge stream of good résumés. You're going to get maybe four or five. You can't run the same play as you did for the other jobs.

But you *can* run a play that will show you who the good candidates are. Maybe a group interview won't be appropriate, because there are so few candidates. Instead, you have candidates wait in the lobby, and you send in various people to engage them on the stupid levels, such as "Did you see a delivery guy up here, because I thought I saw a delivery guy?" You observe their reaction. Do they blow off the employee who is trying to engage them, or do they pay attention? Or you could have an employee approach them and say, "I think I've misplaced some papers in here." Do the candidates try to help the employee find the missing paper? Even the way candidates respond to a question such as "What time is it?" can give you a sense of who they are.

How people behave when they don't think anyone's watching will tell you a lot about where their values are. Then you do the one-on-one for skills, after which applicants have to spend a day with the team so you can figure out if they fit. These are the measures that matter. It's not about studying their résumés, it's not about talking to them on the phone, and it's not just a one-on-one interview in which the interviewer is doing all the talking. It's about having a system that puts culture first in the hiring process.

KEEPING YOUR NEW TALENT

In theory, you've now found someone who has the right values, the right skills, the right cultural fit, and who gets along with your people. How you treat that new hire on the first day and during the first thirty days, sixty days, and six months may determine how long that person stays with you. People tend to make up their mind about how long they're going to stay on the job their first day. How much time have you put in to prepare for your new hire's first day, and how welcome do they feel?

We have new hires start on Tuesdays, around 9:15 a.m. We're prepared to welcome them, not scrambling to get to work. Their first forty-eight to seventy-two hours are tightly scheduled. They get a checklist of one hundred tasks they need to do in the first sixty days to earn their spot with us. These tasks include meeting key personnel, understanding how we handle procedural stuff, learning the pet peeves of the owner, where to park, how to use the kitchen, and how to maximize their experience here. In short, we give them the action steps they must assimilate to become fully fledged members of our team. Why the checklist? Without a checklist, we'd do it differently every time.

If a method that has no checklist is used, cultural assimilation happens inconsistently over an indeterminate period of time. It becomes a version of the telephone game in which a specific message trickles down to a completely different message. The rule might be "Write your name on your lunch," but eighteen people later, it has become "You're going to be fired for eating someone's lunch." That's not good. It's much cleaner to say up front, "Here are all the things you need to know to get along with us." Here are the videos, books, manuals, meetings, training sessions, and people you should learn from to understand how we work here. Lay it all out there on day one. If that scares off some new hires, let them leave.

FIRST DAY CHECKLIST   NAME: _____

Welcome aboard! This First Day Checklist will guide your onboarding process for your first 60 days here. It's your responsibility to ensure that every item is completed and signed off on within the first 60 days. On or around the 60th day of employment, the Founder/President will meet with you to wrap up the Orientation Checklist process. Once this form is completed a final copy will go to you, one copy will go to your manager, and one copy will be kept on file in HR. If you have questions along the way or get stuck at any point, reach out to your manager or HR.

AT A GLANCE

	Owner	Check for Completed	Owner Initials	Date Complete
9:15 am Greeting	Receptionist	☐	_____	_____
9:20 am Tour of 300 10th Ave S	Executive Assistant	☐	_____	_____
10 am HR Orientation	HR Manager	☐	_____	_____
11 am Settle In	HR Manager	☐	_____	_____
12 pm Welcome Lunch	Hiring Manager	☐	_____	_____
2 pm Technical Overview	Hiring Manager	☐	_____	_____
3 pm Facilities Overview	Facilities Coordinator	☐	_____	_____
4 pm First Day Review	Hiring Manager	☐	_____	_____

CHECKLIST FOR THE CHECKLIST

Greeting   Receptionist 9:15 am

- ☐ Take Headshot on Phone
- ☐ Cube/Office Number
- ☐ 3–4 Fun Facts (i.e. alma mater, previous job, hometown, hobbies, pets, etc.)
- ☐ Email photo and info to Communications

Tour of 300 10th Ave S   EA 9:20 am

- ☐ Area of First Impression
- ☐ Wall of Fame
- ☐ CWAC Wall
- ☐ War Hall
- ☐ BetterBookClub Library
- ☐ Brandau Craig Dickerson Timeline
- ☐ Overview of Collaboration
- ☐ Second Floor Landing
- ☐ Back Staircase
- ☐ Smoking Area
- ☐ Studio
- ☐ Client Services
- ☐ Mail Room
- ☐ Evacuation and Tornado Plans
- ☐ Parking
- ☐ Cummins Station

- [ ] Legal Intake Professionals
- [ ] Kitchen & Breakroom
- [ ] IT, Accounting, LIP Client Services
- [ ] FedEx/Mail Drop-Off
- [ ] Hiring Manager's Office
- [ ] Attend Huddle (optional)

HR Orientation   HR Manager 10 am

- [ ] Orientation Checklist
- [ ] Orientation Video
- [ ] 2016 Payroll Schedule
- [ ] 2016 Paid Holidays
- [ ] Perks One-Page
- [ ] Arnie's Loves & Hates
- [ ] Birthday Gift Card Program Handout
- [ ] Sexual Harassment Video/Quiz
- [ ] FMLA & PML Fact Sheets
- [ ] Handbook

Technical Overview   Hiring Manager 2 pm

- [ ] Email Signature Process
- [ ] Calendar How To's
- [ ] Requesting Time Off
- [ ] MLG Central
- [ ] VPN
- [ ] Map Drives
- [ ] Interaction Client/SIP Soft Phone
- [ ] Record Voicemail Message
- [ ] Communication Tools
- [ ] Submit Help Desk Ticket for Printing Setup

Facilities Overview   Facilities Coord. 3 pm

- [ ] Facilities Dept. Handout
- [ ] Visitor Process
- [ ] Chair Instructions
- [ ] Parking Information
- [ ] Building Access
- [ ] Thermostats
- [ ] Review Floor Plan
- [ ] Fill Out Car Info Form

First Day Review   Hiring Manager 4 pm

- [ ] Review First Day Checklist
- [ ] Phone System
- [ ] Q&A
- [ ] HelpDesk
- [ ] Email
- [ ] Review Job Description and Goals
- [ ] Copier/Printer
- [ ] Building Access
- [ ] Parking

60-DAY CHECKLIST

NAME: _____

Welcome aboard! This **60-Day Checklist** will guide your onboarding process for your first 60 days here. It's your responsibility to ensure that every item is completed and signed off on within the first 60 days. On or around the 60th day of employment, the Founder/President will meet with you to wrap up the Orientation Checklist process. Once this form is completed a final copy will go to you, one copy will go to your manager, and one copy will be kept on file in HR. If you have questions along the way or get stuck at any point, reach out to your manager or HR.

AT A GLANCE

		Owner	Check for Completed	Owner Initials	Date Complete
1	**Paylocity Orientation** *(Owner – see "Checklist for the Checklist"; only sign off if all items are covered)* Schedule via email within 10 business days of hire date. • cj/MLG COntact: Bryan (Senior Accountant) • LIP Contact: Tara (Staff Accountant) **Note**: Please have emergency contact info prepared for your orientation.	Accounting Dept.	☐		
2	**Printer Setup** • User Box • Print Text Page	IT Dept.	☐		
3	**FiSH! Orientation** Schedule with Renee via email.	FiSH! Champion	☐		
4	**BetterBookClub Orientation** *(Owner – see "Checklist for the Checklist"; only sign off if all items are covered)* Schedule with Kayla via email.	BBC Champion	☐		
5	**Complete BetterBookClub Profile** *(Following your orientation)* • Upload a profile photo • Add hire date • Tag books you've read	Team Member	☐		
6	**Benefits Orientation (Permanent Only)** Schedule with Carmen via email.	HR Manager	☐		
7	**Enroll or waive benefits (Permanent Only)** *(Following your orientation)*	Team Member	☐		
8	**One-Page Plan Overview**	Hiring Manager	☐		
9	**Have Official Photo Taken** Schedule with Rachel via email.	Multimedia Specialist	☐		
10	**Upload Official Photo to Office 365** *Rachel will send instructions when she sends your photo.*	Hiring Manager	☐		
11	**Send Birthday Gift Card Information** *See Birthday Gift Card Program handout for instructions.*	Team Member	☐		

12 Watch the following   **Team Member**

Found in MLG Central on Camel Culture page
- Core Values Video   Team Member   ☐   _____ _____
- Injury Law 101   Team Member   ☐
- Hot Coffee, Erin Brockovich or A Lawyer Walks
  Into a Bar   Team Member   ☐   _____ _____
- After the Accident   Team Member   ☐   _____ _____
- At least 8 Testimonial spots   Team Member   ☐   _____ _____
- At least 5 culture videos   Team Member   ☐   _____ _____

13 Listen to the following   **Team Member**

Found in MLG Central on Camel Culture page
- Arnie's Interview on Acme Radio   Team Member   ☐   _____ _____
- 7 different intake calls   Team Member   ☐   _____ _____

14 Schedule 60-Day Check In   **Executive**   ☐

Schedule with Alli Durfee on or around your 60-day   **Assistant**
mark.
                                                                                        _____ _____

15 Check-In with Founder/President   **Arnie Malham**   ☐
- The Camel Story
- War Hall
- BetterBookClub Profile
- Review Orientation Checklist
- 60-Day Offer to Leave
                                                                     _____

CHECKLIST FOR THE CHECKLIST

BetterBookClub Orientation   BBC Champion

☐   BetterBookClub.com
☐   Guidelines
☐   Profile
☐   Library
☐   Book Reports
☐   Meetings
☐   Dashboard

Paylocity Orientation   Acct. Dept

☐   How to use Web Time
☐   How to check PTO balance and request time off (LIP)
☐   How to add Emergency Contact Info

This Orientation Checklist is for your reference, but don't just copy it. Make up your own list based on what your people need to know. What I do want you to understand about our list is how specific and thoughtful it is. It doesn't just contain training videos and instruction manuals. It contains enriching tasks and assignments that will help new hires get a comfortable seat on our bus. We want them to watch movies such as *Erin Brockovich* and *A Civil Action* because they speak to the heroic things lawyers can do for the less powerful in our society. We have them read books such as *FiSH!* to teach them our philosophy on building morale and being a team member. We're giving them a view into the collective psyche of our company. Once we hand the new employees their sixty-day checklist, it's up to them to complete every task we want them to accomplish in the first sixty days.

AT THE SIXTY-DAY MARK

When new team members complete their first sixty days, I personally talk to them, go through the highlights and the checklist, ask them a few questions, tell them what's important to me, and congratulate them for making it through the first milestone. Then I give them a piece of paper with these two statements for them to ponder:

1. I like everything I've seen. Everything you've told me would happen, happened. I'm excited about my job, and I'm prepared to gain some permanency in my tenure here.
   or

2. I understand that you will give me two weeks' pay, no questions asked, if I just say this is not for me.

I say, "Please take this home and talk to your significant other, family, or pet about this. Check one of the boxes, sign it, and bring it back to your boss tomorrow." Signing the sixty-day agreement is by no means meant to be the fulfillment of a contract. It doesn't commit new employees to anything. It simply and powerfully sets the tone in their mind that they are now fully fledged team members. Plus, I get to say on day one, "If you're not happy here after sixty days, I'll give you two weeks' pay to leave." I've never had to, but I would.

You have to like and respect the people you work with. Finding the right people requires more of you than just saying, "We're open for business. Come work here." It requires a PR plan for attracting good candidates and an efficient plan for identifying the right fit. Once we get them, we do everything we can to help them be successful.

WELCOME AFTER SIXTY DAYS

We believe in continuing to let people know that we value them. We have important milestones built into our culture that celebrate seniority and expertise. After five years, employees get their very own company-specific varsity letter jacket, which they wear with pride. Why five years? According to Malcolm Gladwell's book *Outliers*, ten thousand hours is how long it takes to get great at what you do. Ten thousand hours, at forty hours per week, adds up to about five years at work. The letter jacket signifies that you're now a tenured veteran, or a *letterman*, as we say. The letterman jackets are in our company colors, embroidered with our company's mascot, and the year you started is on the sleeve. This probably isn't the jacket that you're going to go show off at your next fancy social gathering, but you can't get it anywhere else, and you'll never throw it away, because you earned it. People display them on their office chairs to signify their status (and for a quick source of warmth when the AC goes haywire). When we refer to a department with a lot of veterans, we say, "There are a lot of jackets in that department."

These days, ten years is a long time to work at the same place. At our organization, we view it as a huge commitment that deserves a fitting award. We give our ten-year veterans a Rolex. Everyone appreciates a Rolex. Some people don't wear watches, most don't turn down a Rolex.

For folks who make it past the fifteen-year milestone, we put a lot of thought into what would be an appropriate recognition of that kind of dedication. We came up with the notion of giving them a great experience. We ask them to talk to their significant others or families and decide on a trip they could only take if we were to help them out with the costs. We sent our first fifteen-year veteran to Ireland. Our second took his family to Orlando to experience all the parks. Our third took her significant other to a resort in Mexico. And our fourth is headed to Italy for the trip of a lifetime. We want them all to have an experience that they will never forget.

Our orientation video tells incoming hires all about these rewards because we want our new people to know we value their time with us, and these are experiences that might be different from anywhere else they've worked. We hope it keeps our workplace worth talking about and one where people want to stay.

All that said, I don't look at turnover as a problem as much as I look at it as growth. We are all on our way somewhere. Sometimes we can provide people with a worthwhile opportunity for growth, and sometimes they need to go somewhere else.

My personal belief is that I want to celebrate everyone's success no matter where it happens. If employees go because they can experience a better path somewhere else, that's great, and if they stay because we create an opportunity for them, that's great too.

I think client satisfaction is 100 percent tied to employee satisfaction. If your employees are happy and excited, your clients are more likely to be happy and excited. I wake up most every day and say, "What can I do to help my team do a better job?" I need to have my team waking up every day wondering how they can help our clients do a better job. I want our clients to wake up every day feeling really appreciative of their partnership with us. Think of the alternative: I wake up every day griping about my employees not listening to me. My employees never know what our clients want and wake up every day wishing they worked somewhere else. Our clients wake up every day trying to find someone to replace me as their service provider. That's not a good scenario.

A happy team member is a good recruiting tool. If team members are enthusiastic about going to work and have winning stories to tell about work, other good people will hear about it and want to come here. We love it when they post stuff about the company on their social media sites. Because we're a fun place to work, we're big on sharing what we're doing. We give tours to anyone who asks. We will walk them through our office and show them the highlights of the culture, the business, KPIs, and we'll do our best to tell them why we do what we do, and how we do what we do. We share very openly. When it comes to knocking culture and business out of the park, we're probably a B or B-. We're certainly not the best culture I've ever seen, but we're doing all we can, and we are an open book.

There are so many good ideas, so many opportunities to improve and learn and shake things up. I'm not too proud to borrow a successful idea and maybe try to find ways to improve on it for our purposes. Someone recently told me she uses a "culture calendar" to help her plan this kind of stuff, and it blew my mind. What a great idea! I'll be ripping that one off.

You've just got to find ways to take what you're doing and build upon it. If someone isn't thinking about new ideas every day, your culture will get stale. It will become staged. It will become "We do this because we've always done it," as opposed to "This is awesome."

And don't be afraid to rip off and duplicate. Only an idiot would waste time trying to reinvent the wheel. The trick is to refine the design and get it spinning faster.

Business is hard.
Having the wrong people makes it impossible.

CHAPTER SEVEN

DO IT WRONG, MAKE IT BETTER, GET IT RIGHT

You want to know how committed I am to doing it wrong on the way to getting it right? That mantra has defined my entire career, a thirty-year résumé of peaks and valleys, starts and stops, detours and drag races. I've loved (nearly) every minute of it. One of my favorite things about being an entrepreneur is swapping war stories with like-minded business maniacs. Here are a few of my deepest entrepreneurial battle scars, presented in a way that I hope will help you.

BIRTH OF CJ ADVERTISING

I didn't set out to be a culture expert or an advertising magnate. In college, I studied banking and finance. Coming from a small town, I thought finance seemed very *big town* (Wall Street and brokers and all that). Heck, I was good at math, and I thought this could be my ticket out.

But when I graduated, brokerages weren't hiring. Banks were. Fate brought me to First American National Bank in Nashville, Tennessee. My first boss, Martha Elzen, patiently taught me how to compare a host of specific business indices for one business to its industry averages and find anything above or below the average. In other words, I was analyzing what we now call outliers, looking for management by exception. I didn't know it, but that banking job turned out to be the perfect preparation for what providence had in store for me.

After a year of banking, I missed exercising the sales skills I'd learned from working with my dad at the hardware store. When a local TV station was looking to add a class of greenhorns to its sales team, I jumped at the opportunity. But when I got there, the office was going through a renovation and didn't have a desk for me. They stuck me in the production area, two floors down. At first, I thought, *This is not cool. I'm not going to be around my team or my boss. How am I going to learn how to do my job?*

But it ended up being way cool and helped me develop my secret weapon in sales. Thanks to proximity, I learned how commercials were made, got chummy with some of the production staff, and earned a few favors. When they finally turned me loose to sell, I was able to work package deals that even veteran salespeople couldn't do. When I got a new client, I'd magically get a commercial produced and on the air in a snap. I was killing my sales quotas (arguably because I was given the wrong desk). In sales, when you get hot, as I was, your bosses start giving you more leads. One day, I got a lead that would change my life. It was a law firm.

Back then, most of the experienced reps and slick ad agencies didn't handle legal advertising. They didn't understand the business and had no appreciation of the value of the service. Fortunately, I was too young and stupid to know better. The older reps sluffed these PI leads off to me, and I loved it. After two years, I had four PI accounts advertising on TV. What I noticed fairly quickly was that the firms and ad agencies representing them had no idea what they were doing. It was killing me.

The last straw came in the form of a particular ad agency that was being a huge pain in my ass. The staff would hold up payment, drag their feet on contract approvals, or find some other way to give us a hard time, all the while spinning the problem to cast blame on the law firm. One day, I'd had enough. I went rogue and visited the client myself. This was highly unorthodox, but I felt it was the right thing to do.

I asked the attorneys if they were aware that their ad agency was making them look as if they couldn't pay their bills. I told them I thought they were getting a bad deal. The attorneys were shocked but very receptive to what I had to say.

About that time, another firm, Hughes & Coleman from Kentucky, had begun to establish a market presence in Nashville. They had experienced the same problem I had discovered: that their industry was short on quality advertising help. During a sales meeting, J. Marshall Hughes, a name partner at the firm, asked me the magic question "Is there a better way?" That's how I recognized the opportunity in the niche that became our business. I started helping Hughes & Coleman with its advertising, and J. Marshall taught me the business of personal injury law.

As you can probably guess, this kind of moonlighting got me fired. The bad news was I was unprepared to start my own business. The good news was I didn't have a choice. It was sink-or-swim time.

cj Advertising was born with one flagship client, and a few other up-and-comers (Bob Crumley from Greensboro, North Carolina, and Bill Berg from Alameda, California). We started building their advertising, which built their practices, which, in turn, built their brands and eventually made them advertising giants and household names in their respective markets.

From my banking days, I was a stickler for measuring everything. When new clients came along to kick the tires, I had solid analytics to back up our creative work. I was running an ad agency with a banker's mentality—and it was working. Four clients became six, six clients became twelve, and twelve clients became twenty-four. Slowly but surely, we learned that sustained success was about having the right operation. Having the right operation meant having the right culture. And the process of slow growth gave us time to do it wrong on the way to getting it right.

The growth and sustained success of cj Advertising was the primer I needed. It convinced me I had a secret ingredient for entrepreneurial success: healthy and regular doses of failure. And here they are…

THE FINE ART OF FAILING UP

Failing up is not the art of not making mistakes; it's the art of making mistakes that push you forward. Here are a few of my favorite failing-up examples on the entrepreneurial level. This is the kind of failure you should be experiencing.

USINJURYLAWYERS.COM: YEE HAW! WATCH THIS!

Back in the late '90s when consumer dot-coms were still in the embryonic stage, our Minnesota client, Geoff Gempeler, came up with this concept called USInjuryLawyers.com. We saw it as a web-based portal for lawyers. Consumers who needed an injury lawyer would go to USInjuryLawyers.com, where they would select their state and their city and then choose a lawyer who could help them. We were convinced this was the idea of the century—so convinced, in fact, that my partner and I actually bought big white cowboy hats and wore them in a booth at the American Trial Lawyer Association Convention in San Francisco. We were so advanced that we were doomed to fail. Two-thirds of the country didn't even have an e-mail account yet.[1] We had to pitch the concept, explain the Internet, and convince cynical law firms it was all going to work. Here we were, at the center of the tech universe, my East Tennessee redneck partner and a big tall Arab, in cowboy hats, looking like effing morons, and telling lawyers, "It's lawyers on the inn-turr-net. It's gold!"

Fail? Yes, but the experience enabled us to get ahead of the curve with online marketing for lawyers. Now our in-house interactive team is a huge part of our success.

DIVERSIFICATION: GOOD FOR THE PORTFOLIO, BAD FOR BUSINESS

After a few years of cj Advertising, we thought we were pretty hot stuff. So we started another, more general ad company, cj Adworks. We didn't appreciate the extent to which our success at cj had been predicated on our niche status. Our creativity wasn't quite as good or as valuable as our in-depth understanding of our business sector. It was another failure but one that caused us to refocus on being the best within our area of expertise. Since then, we've never taken our eye off the ball.

That experience got us back in the mind-set of "go with what we know," which led to an offshoot for the agency called Stuff 4 Lawyers. We were trying to sell a marketing tool kit for lawyers, including on-hold messages, training videos, client-education videos, among other tools. But our prospective customers thought we were selling pens, sticky pads, and business cards.

---

1   "Internet Users (per 100 people)," The World Bank, http://data.worldbank.org/indicator/IT.NET.USER.P2?page=3.

Wump wump.

What we did learn, however, was that the hardest thing in marketing is overcoming perception. Rather than fight it, accept it and make it work for you.

THE NEAR-DEATH OF LIP

I've already touched on why LIP was formed and that it continues to be an incredibly successful intake and triage service for law firms. What I didn't tell you is that after our first two hours of operation, we had to halt indefinitely. Two hours! You're probably wondering, "How hard could it be to answer phone calls, ask questions, and forward the answers to law firms?" Funny you ask. Because that's what we were thinking when we started LIP! Two hours later, we had our answer: it's pretty damn hard. We were so bad and knew so little about what we were doing I had to call the clients (tail between my legs) and say, "We have to close. We can't do this." All four of them, Terry Bryant, J. Marshall Hughes, Bob Crumley, and Carter Mario, encouraged me to take what we had learned and build on it. They all said they believed in my partner and me, and they looked forward to us trying again soon. We refocused, retrained, and reopened four weeks later. We've never closed since. LIP currently has over a hundred team members answering calls for over 275 law firm clients across the country. All we do is inbound and outbound calls for personal injury law firms. As of mid-2016, we've processed more than 2.5 million intakes. That's what I mean by getting it wrong on the way to getting it right!

PRELAW, PREMED: WHAT'S THE DIFFERENCE?

Our momentum with LIP inspired one of our top clients, Carter Mario of Connecticut, to bring us another really promising idea based on intakes. His firm was getting a lot of calls from people who thought they might be the victims of medical malpractice and were requesting a legal consultation. Ordinarily, a lot of calls for legal services would be a good thing, but the challenge firms face when dealing with med mal calls is separating the wheat from the chaff. In the PI business, if you get a hundred phone calls from people claiming malpractice, you'll find only one or two viable cases. To qualify as a medical malpractice case, someone has to sustain some sort of permanent injury caused by some deviation in the care that the doctor performed. Figuring out what *might* qualify entails a tremendously complex vetting process that you can't determine with *yes* and *no* questions. This process requires long conversations about sensitive and sophisticated data. Valuable attorney time was flying out the window.

The solution was to have someone who understood medical issues participate in the initial phone call. We formed a company called MedView Services, a network of registered nurses whose job was to listen to the caller, ask pertinent questions, and determine if the case met the medical criteria to be considered by the firm. Everything about the business seemed like a win: efficiency for the law firm, opportunity for nurses to make extra money, and a more expedient answer for the potential plaintiff. With our success from taking calls at LIP and knowledge of the legal industry, what could go wrong? We proved, however, that even when a concept makes sense and everything goes right, simply not having enough scale means the business just can't gain velocity. We simply could not find enough med-mal law firms to scale the idea. The firms that did try out our company found that our solution helped them focus on improving their internal triage methods, which strengthened their trust in us.

That's a lot of failure—and a lot of benefit gained. We did all we could with everything possible to make these ideas work because they were worth doing wrong. In the end, we're better for it. If you're a budding or experienced entrepreneur, you probably have a similarly high tolerance for risk. That's good. That means you're ready to proceed to the next chapter.

**Business is hard.
If you are not getting something wrong,
you're not doing it right.**

CHAPTER EIGHT

NEVER GIVE UP

THIS IS HOW WE LIVE

One Saturday morning, I was in the living room relaxing, watching a little *SportsCenter*, hanging out, and waiting for some football to come on. A friend calls. "Hey, what's going on? I need to come by. I want to drop off something. You mind if I come by for a minute and grab a cup of coffee?"

I'm like, "Great. Come on by."

I put the phone down. My wife walks by.

"Hey, who was that?" she asks.

"It's John. He's going to come by. We're going to hang out and drink a cup of coffee."

"Okay." She takes a shirt off the couch, picks up the half-read paper, starts straightening out some stuff on the counter, and asks me if I'm through with my cup. She's cleaning up.

"Honey, what are you doing?"

"I'm cleaning up."

"Why are you cleaning up?"

"Because John's coming over."

"It's *John*. He's been over here a hundred times! Why do you care?"

"Arnie, I'm cleaning up because I don't want him to think we live this way."

Pause.

This is *how we live,* I say to myself. "You're right, honey. Let me help you out."

The stories I'm sharing with you aren't about how I remember us living. They aren't about how I wish we had lived. They're how we *actually* live *now.* Some stuff works, and some stuff doesn't. When you discover what makes your company better, make sure you can sustain it—*because it's how you live.*

TWENTY YEARS TO BECOMING AN OVERNIGHT SUCCESS

As a business owner for twenty-plus years, I don't get to tell you stories about how I remember the company working. I have to tell you stories about how the company *is* working. I make fun of a lot of practicing business coaches because they aren't running companies. They're running coaching operations, which tell other companies how to run their business. But coaches don't have a business, so even the gurus of the business world aren't gurus of the business world, because they don't actually have a business they're running. They get to remember what my father would always call "the good old days."

My dad would always say, "Let me tell you something, son. There wasn't anything good about the good old days. Before air conditioning, we used to sweat ourselves to sleep every night and wake soaking wet in the morning. We used to freeze our butts off in the winter because the cold came right through the house most winters. We had to walk everywhere." In his recollection, there was nothing much good about the good old days, except what people choose to forget or choose to remember.

I think running a company is like that. I've been running this company for over twenty years, and it's so easy to look back and go, "Oh, it was so much easier when we only had fifteen employees. It was so much easier when we didn't have all these bills to pay, or we didn't have this big building."

But it wasn't.

There's no time in business where it was "so much easier." I defy you to find an entrepreneur of a company of any size and at any point in its development who will tell you, "This is easy." It's not. Business is hard.

I meet people who say, "Oh, you guys are great. I see you every-where. You were lucky to find that niche." That's what they say, and they mean it.

I reply, "Yeah, real lucky. It only took fifteen years to get some momentum."

That's because, to quote Susan Scott (*Fierce Conversations*), every great company happens "gradually and then all of a sudden." The other day, I read a *Forbes* article, "The World's Most Valuable Brands." That list mostly comprises twelve-, fifteen-, twenty-, and even fifty-year-old companies. It's hard to find one top brand that could be considered an overnight success. We're talkin' about brands such as Apple, Microsoft, McDonald's, Coca-Cola, BMW, and General Electric. And the ones that *did* experience meteoric beginnings (such as Facebook or Google) have to fight like hell just to stay on top. No one would guess that. But there it is. Overnight successes, when they do happen, tend to fizzle out after a couple of years; they just don't have the staying power. Success is not obtained quickly. It is as Jim Collins put in in *Great by Choice,* a methodical march, a willingness to get it wrong over the years in order to get it right. Once you've done it wrong enough times, you'll better understand and remember how to do it right. That's the way failure happens. It's the way success happens. If you think it's any other thing, you just haven't been in business long enough.

DON'T BE A WUSS

I got an e-mail recently that read, "Hey, we heard you do some cool stuff with culture. Would you consider speaking at our annual event?"

I replied, "I'm honored that you'd ask. What I do onstage is inspire optimism and creative strategy for building culture. I encourage people to open up to a creative and optimistic culture. I'd like to know who the audience is. If you're bringing me a bunch of people who don't have the ability to change, then don't have me speak to them, because all I'm going to do is depress them."

I went to visit a company in Pittsburgh at the invitation of the owner, who had asked me to come and talk to his staff about the things we were doing. I told them all about birthday cards for the whole family and about the envelopes with cash prizes. I told them about BetterBookClub and paying people to read. He almost threw me out because he wasn't willing to do any of that stuff. It was like taking a bunch of people from former East Germany, showing them West Germany for six months, and then making them go back home. It was terrible.

You can't just *want* a better culture. You have to create an environment that gives you a better culture. Culture reflects leadership. Culture reflects leadership. *Culture reflects leadership.* And leadership is knowing what you want and creating a strategy to get there.

Susan Scott talks about the "squid eye," a great story about divers who developed the skill of being able to spot the eyes of squids hiding in the sand, deep below the surface. If you're not looking for a squid's eye or don't know what to look for, a squid's eye looks like a pebble in the sand. Once you know how to spot it, you can find it. Experienced divers can harvest squid easily because they can spot that eye. Inexperienced divers would take forever because they don't know what they're looking for.

It's the same with your culture. If something's not happening right, you have to recognize it. If the reports aren't coming regularly, if you're not hearing people mentioning them, if you haven't seen a result, you have to be tuned into that problem. You have to say, "Wait, I'm used to seeing it this way. Now I'm seeing it that way. What changed?"

Your business will grow. People will change. Your culture *must* change with it. Train yourself to spot the squid eye so you know what needs to be fixed.

THE ENTREPRENEURIAL ROLLER COASTER: MUST BE OLD ENOUGH TO RIDE

Recently, while judging a best-in-business contest, I was able to visit three different companies on the same day, each of them at a different stage on what Cameron Herold calls the entrepreneurial roller coaster.

The first stage is like that moment on the roller coaster when you haven't reached the top of the arc yet, and all you see is blue sky, and all you feel is excitement. That's kind of a great place to be; it's exhilarating.

Then, as you continue this entrepreneurial journey, you get to the second stage where you have crested the top of the roller coaster. You are now pointed downward. You realize you can't see blue sky anymore. The acceleration is pulling your stomach through your throat, and your fear is like nothing you've ever experienced. You've only moved thirty feet, but the angle has changed, the speed has increased, everything is different. Now you are terrified. And that's a unique place in the entrepreneurial journey. You're really getting what you asked for: employees are complaining, clients are complaining, the landlord's complaining, and expenses are going up. Everything you thought you knew gets thrown out the window as you plummet downward on this roller coaster.

Then there's this third stage, where the roller coaster comes back in contact with the rails. You start to plane out to the bottom. You can see the sky again, but you're still going really fast. You're still scared. But you now know what you didn't know before. You have confidence that it's going to be okay because you can tell you're not going to die.

Of the three businesses I visited, each of the three leaders was at a different place in his overall entrepreneurial journey. The first one had read all the right books, was doing all the right things, and was extremely enthusiastic, but he still didn't know what he didn't know.

The second one had found himself accelerating at such a rapid pace that he literally didn't know whether to order more furniture, fire someone, hire someone, go to the bank, talk to a customer, or vomit. It was all happening at once, and you could see the panic in his face.

The third one had found a place where his business worked, and he was confident that while there were going to be challenges, he had enough experience to traverse the next few years of his business.

If you took any one of those guys out of his company and stuck him in the environment of one of the other leaders, he would fail because he wouldn't fit the culture. When the leader is experiencing one of these cycles, the entire company can be going through that same cycle. How the entrepreneur reacts to those cycles will determine how much success the company has.

DON'T EAT BIRTHDAY CAKE ON A ROLLER COASTER!

The roller-coaster stage you're in dictates the business decisions you make. It should also be reflected in your culture. My favorite way to illustrate how culture evolves along with your business is cj Advertising's birthday cake policy:

"NO BIRTHDAY CAKE ALLOWED."

Sounds kind of stingy and buzzkillish? It's not. The ban on birthday cakes started soon after we entered roller-coaster "stage two" as a reaction to how we had behaved during roller-coaster "stage one." When we were a smaller group, every time someone had a birthday, that someone got a cake. We'd all gather around and sing, "Happy birthday to you…" It worked when we had three people. It worked with eight people. It stopped working at fifteen or twenty people because it felt as if we were singing "Happy (%$#*in') birthday" and having cake every (effin') day. If I was in the middle of something, I didn't want to stop and have an awkward birthday party. No one else really did either.

So we started trying different ways to celebrate without songs and baked cliché. We tried giving people a half day off. But then we had people saying, "Well, I don't want to take a half day today," or "My birthday was on Saturday. Do I still get a half day off?" or "I'm not going to do it today. I'm going to use it another day. If I'm really gone for the full day, does that count as a half day?" Meanwhile, the roller coaster was speeding down the rails at 100 mph. It became a problem.

We found a great new way to do birthdays. We started sending people a $50 gift certificate for their birthdays, with a card that read, "Hey, Happy Birthday. Glad you're able to celebrate it. Do something for yourself." That was good, but the next step was better. We started sending their *spouses* a birthday card with $50, and later, we started sending their kids a birthday card with $25. That's been a huge hit. We want the family to support the teammate here. We want to honor people on their birthdays, and we want to do it in a way that fits our company, now cruising at the third stage of the roller coaster.

That's what I mean about a culture that evolves.

BUSINESS IS HARD

Business is hard. Running one without an intentional culture is harder, exhausting, and no fun. It'll suck the life right out of you. The only advantage your company has is people. And the only advantage you can give them is a strong, sustainable culture. Don't be the guy who works people until they can't work anymore. Don't be the guy who's the only one who can do it right. Don't be the guy who is so caught up in his own value that he doesn't allow other people to reach their potential. Be the guy who delivers the culture that powers the engine that's your business.

Embrace failure, demand growth, get it wrong, make it right, and never give up.

Business is hard.
Remove "can't" from your vocabulary.

IN CLOSING . . .

Here's a riddle for you:

There are four seagulls sitting on the dock. Three decide to leave. How many seagulls are left?

Answer: Four. Why? Because deciding to leave and leaving are two different things.

I don't pretend to know everything about culture, because creating one is an organic process in which I'm still very much engaged. I do know a little about human habits, though—enough to know that after reading this book, you're likely going to R&D the ideas in it. You'll go back to your committee, board, partner, and/or team members, who will proceed to give you the eighteen to twenty-four reasons your ideas are not going to work.

Don't listen, or you'll end up like the seagulls on the dock.

Accept the fact that you will have to implement some bad ideas to get to some good ones. Everyone told me that paying people to read was stupid. *Everyone.* Now the same people are saying, "Oh yes, I always thought that was a good idea." Bullshit. They told me it was stupid. As a business owner, you need the conviction to say, "I'm going to try stuff that other people tell me is stupid because it's worth doing wrong."

Whenever I talk to a group about Camel Culture, there's usually at least one guy in the audience who refuses to accept that culture reflects leadership. This type of person says, "That won't work for us. Only successful companies do that," or "When I get good people, I'll have a better culture." Of course, to their own detriment, these guys are right.

Thank you for reading. I hope I've helped you understand the importance of culture in business. If I haven't, I'll keep trying till I get it right.

AFTERWORD

OUR CULTURE IS IN THE CAMEL

As I've said before, I grew up in small-town Arkansas, but my ethnicity is Lebanese. I attended college at Ole Miss. About my third day as a freshman on campus, I was walking around with my new friends when a battered pickup truck pulled up alongside us. This guy leaned out the window, glared at us, and yelled, "Hey you! Go home, camel jockey!"

I looked back at my new buddies and said, "Who's he talking to?"

They said, "He's talking to you, dumbass."

I said, "Oh, I'm not a camel jockey. I'm a redneck from Arkansas."

They thought that was the funniest thing in the world. From that moment forward, they started calling me camel jockey. I was done. I was camel jockey. Everywhere we went, my friends introduced me as their "camel-jockey friend," which they knew half-irritated me but which I also thought was pretty funny. (Side note: there are actually no camels in Lebanon, where my family is from, or in Brinkley, Arkansas, either.) Why get mad? Optimistically, I knew there had to be a purpose. It was all great. If that's what I needed to be, I was happy to be camel jockey, just hanging out with my redneck friends from Texas at Ole Miss. I got so used to it I voluntarily carried it forward into my professional life. I even named my ad agency after it: the "cj" in cj Advertising stands for camel jockey.

Now, whenever visitors or new hires ask, "What's up with the camel?" I tell them the story about that redneck yelling at me back in college. People love that story because it takes an insult and turns it into a positive. We took something unique, something that was different, and we made it our own. This book follows the same principle: take what could turn into a negative, and mold it into a positive.

APPENDIX I

REFERENCED AUTHORS AND LEADERS

Joe Calloway (Forward)
Be the Best at What Matters Most

Cameron Herold (page 4, 109)
Double Double

John DiJulius (page 7, 51)
Customer Service Revolution

Steven Kotler (page 17)
Rise of Superman

Verne Harnish (page 24)
Scaling Up

Matthew Kelly (page 41)
The Dream Manager

Jack Daly (page 42, 45)
Hyper Sales Growth

Stephen C. Lundin and Harry Paul
(page 47, 48, 90, 92)
FiSH!

Rory Vaden (page 51)
Procrastinate on Purpose

Larry Linne (page 53)
Make the Noise Go Away

Malcolm Gladwell (page 93)
Outliers

Jim Collins (page 107)
Great by Choice

Susan Scott (page 107, 108)
Fierce Conversations

APPENDIX II

ARNIE-ISMS:
THE THINGS I FIND MYSELF REPEATING THROUGHOUT MY MANUSCRIPT OF LIFE

"IF IT'S WORTH DOING, IT'S WORTH DOING WRONG"
(page 2 & the premise of the entire book)
This phrase has become my signature approach to business and life as well as my most frequent advice to others on their unique journeys.

"BUSINESS IS HARD"
(page 4, 107, & 112)
I can't say it enough, it is just is. Saying otherwise is like telling your kids they're smart or talented rather than connecting their hard work to success. "Smart and talented" kids can often disappoint and quit when "hard working" kids take their place on the podium.

"CULTURE REFLECTS LEADERSHIP"
(page 7, 52, 108, 113)
First heard from John DiJulius in his 2007 presentation at our annual client conference, this truth is typically ignored by businesses waiting to fail and embraced by businesses who are playing to win.

"TELL ME MORE"
(page 17)
More often than not, the most universally perfect response ever.

"THIS IS HOW WE LIVE!"
(page 105, 106)
There are stories we tell others and truths we know to be so, but you can always see a person's priorities through the lens of how they spend their time and their money. My quest is to continually eliminate the delta between my truth and my story.

"TWENTY YEARS TO BECOME AN OVERNIGHT SUCCESS"
(page 106)
Great brands, great people, great families typically all seem easy, but in reality all take time... lots of time. Life's not a lottery ticket, buckle in for the long haul.

"GRADUALLY, THEN ALL OF A SUDDEN"
(page 107)
Discovered in Susan Scott's "Fierce Conversations", this answers the popular questions, "How did you get into Lawyer Advertising?", "How did you build this great culture?", "How did you and your wife raise your children?", "How did you (fill in the blank)"... the answer is almost inevitably the same.

"WE'VE DONE IT WRONG ENOUGH TO FIGURE OUT HOW TO DO IT RIGHT"
(page 107–108)
My response to most compliments about my businesses.

VISUAL CULTURE

 **Morale Score**

Total comments received since March 2007 : 1827

8.14
May 2016 Score

82%
May 2016 Participation Rate

Since starting the morale surveys in 2007, monthly morale scores and participation rates have been updated and posted monthly in our war hall.

MORALE

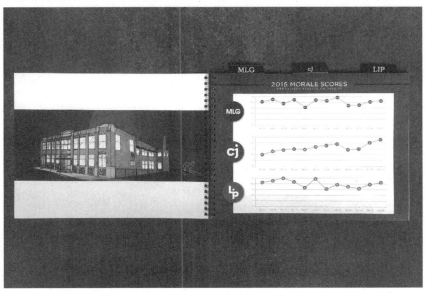

Every year, in addition to transparently publishing all scores, comments and responses on the web, we publish a book reviewing all this information and include pictures of good times enjoyed. Multiple copies of the book are available for anyone to browse in our lobby or breakroom throughout the year.

MORALE

PUBLISHED ANNUALLY SINCE 2009

MORALE BOOK
2015

Comment # 1649 Remember the Golden Rule, please, and give a little grace to coworkers. You have no idea the workload of others, especially those in different departments. Before you judge or criticize just take a moment. Is that person pulling the load of three others, or maybe you don't even know what they do besides "your stuff?" If a mistake is made, address it but show some mercy. Good people may leave just because they're having a stressful season and coworkers/leadership aren't understanding.

Thanks. I feel better having that off my chest. (5) We wholeheartedly agree, and this comment sparked a great conversation regarding the potential disconnect between co-workers. There are gaps in knowledge of other departments and understanding of each other's workload, and as a small organization, we need to make a collective effort to close it. Thank you for bringing this to our attention.

cj FEBRUARY2015

Total Number of Participants – 40 (71%) **7.85** Morale Average

Comment # 1650 Really appreciate the flexibility with the ice and snow days. I know in the past we've had a more strict policy on taking PTO for these situations, but this really allowed everyone to stay home and be safe. We should never have to risk our lives for fear of losing personal days, so thank you! (9) Everyone's response to the critical weather confirmed that trust and respect is a much better path to the working environment we are targeting. Thank you for being a great, innovative, and resourceful team.

Comment # 1651 Thank you for keeping us safe during the ice storm. We appreciate the capability to work from home. (9) You're welcome!

Comment # 1652 Thank you for letting us work from home during the snow/ice storm! It was actually a nice change of pace working from my house. (9) Thank you for helping prove that "Work's not where you are, it's what you do."

Gnash hung out with Preds Pride Day

MORALE

EDUCATION

An annual recap of our team's training and education opportunities are proudly displayed in our lobby so that all visitors (clients, vendors, and potential team members) know how focused we are on growing our team.

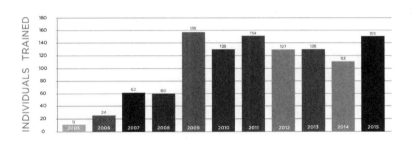

TOTAL INVESTED SINCE 2005:
$522,958

EDUCATION

BETTER BOOK CLUB

When you've paid out as much as we have for reading, sharing the amount, the team's favorite books, and the most active readers seems like a natural. Find a way to get books into the the the brains of your team.

Our BetterBookClub champion ensures our typically themed BetterBookClub meetings are energetic, informative, and well worth attending.

CAMELS IN CULTURE

Several times a year, our camels suit up and deliver smiles in the forms of beer, cookies, hot chocolate, candy, and sometimes song to team members throughout the building.

Everyone is having a jolly ole time as we celebrate Christmas in July in costume, complete with camels delivering cookies and tidings of joy. Yes, that's my partner Jimmy, our COO Chris, and me dressed as Elf 1, Elf 2, and Santa respectively. Big events are unavoidable.

DOG & KID FRIENDLY

We are uber proud that our workplace is both dog and kid friendly. Check out all the smiling faces.

DOG & KID FRIENDLY

DOG & KID FRIENDLY

DOG & KID FRIENDLY

BIRTHDAY & THANK YOU CARDS

Every team member, team member spouse, and team member kid enjoys a
birthday gift card. The cost is fractional compared to the payoff.

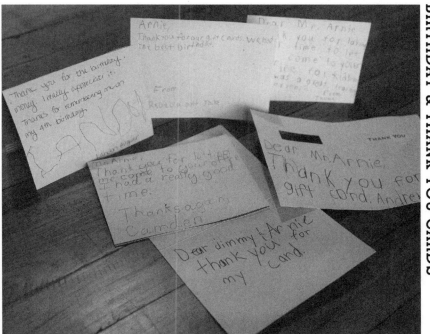

BIRTHDAY & THANK YOU CARDS

The company provides branded thank you cards. Team members provide the continual recognition. The resulting displays of appreciation throughout the workplace are contagiously inspiring.

FREE FRESH FRUIT

Strategically located throughout the building, when team members need energy…we give it to them in the form of year round fresh fruit!!!

FREE FRESH FRUIT

5 YEAR JACKETS

At 5 years, team members have put in about 10,000 hours. They've proven that they are knowledgeable, skilled, and respected by teammates and clients alike. The 'letterman' jacket is meant to distinguish them as the leaders they are within the company.

5 YEAR JACKETS

Nominated by peers, our team generates hundreds of "rocks" a month to each other. From all submitted, 10 are publically named in staff meetings and given a 'thanks for bustin your hump' envelope. Eight envelopes contain $10, one contains $20, and one contains $100.

TEAM MEMBER RECOGNITION

TEAM MEMBER RECOGNITION

155

TEAM MEMBER RECOGNITION

Via banners, video display, and posters…our goal is constant visual recognition of our rock stars throughout the organization.

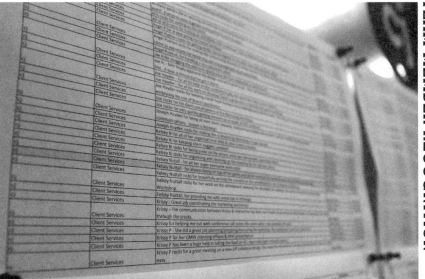

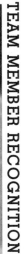

Hundreds of nominations for recognition are generated monthly. All are sorted, displayed, and then distributed monthly. This is yet another version of perpetual cultural energy in the workplace.

CAMEL CULTURE

Our mascot is a camel. Every part of our culture that makes us unique is displayed inside this camel, and this poster is displayed throughout our office including our main lobby.

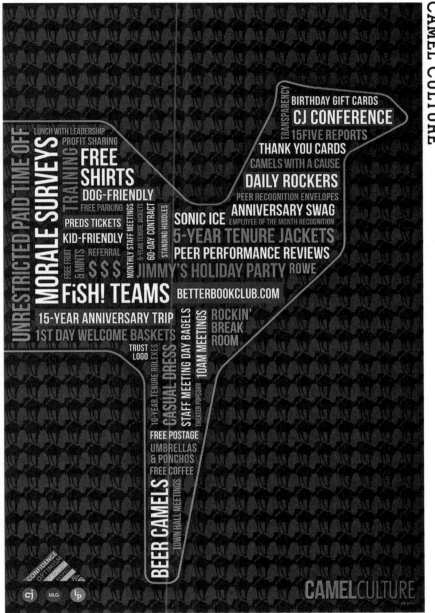

Timing is Everything.